Things I Wish My Teacher Knew About Me

Thing I Wish My Teacher Knew About Me

JOSEPH MATHEWS

CREATE SPACE PUBLISHING

Charleston, SC

CreateSpace Publishing
Charleston, SC

First Paperback printing 2015

©Joseph Mathews

Printed in the United States of America

About Joseph

Joseph Mathews is a nationally known speaker, best known for his "Edutainment" approach to education. As an artist and expert in student and family engagement, Joseph has performed for students all over the country and conducted countless professional developments for teachers centered around student and family engagement. Joseph is the author of four other books: *The Dropout, Wrestling for My Life, Me and My Homies*, and *Why Do Boys Make Girls Cry?* These books are used in schools and classrooms around the country to help foster students motivation to learn, to teach life skills and leadership development, encourage and making better and smarter choices. Joseph has a Bachelor of Arts in Psychology from Langston University, a Master of Arts in Family and Community Education from Columbia University Teachers College and is currently pursuing his Doctoral degree in Urban Education with a concentration in Student, Family and Community Engagement at Columbia University Teachers College.

To book Joseph for workshops, book discussions, book signings, professional development seminars, assemblies, and conferences:

Josephmathews.com
jdm2193@tc.columbia.edu
Phone: 202-702-5262
Find me on Facebook and follow me on Twitter
@josephmathews40

Books can be purchased on Amazon.com
The Dropout
Me and My Homies
Wrestling for My Life
Why Do Boys Make Girls Cry
Things I Wish My Teacher Knew About Me

Dedication

While in the last stages of finishing this book my life was forever changed. The night of March 2, 2015, I sat in class at Columbia University Teachers College in New York City where I am working on my Doctorate in Urban Education, when a deep pain came over me. For some reason I had been sick all day, but could not understand why. As the night went on the pain worsened. One hour after class ended my oldest brother Anthony called to break me the news. With tears in his voice he informed me that his oldest son and my closest nephew Steven, who was more like my brother, had just been murdered back in Texas.

That moment will forever be frozen in time, as me and my brother cried together on the phone, both in disbelief that Steven was gone. For years now, I have spoken around the country to thousands of broken hearted students on the verge of giving up, and dispirited teachers ready to throw in the towel Nothing has been more difficult than standing in front of my broken hearted family and friends at my nephews funeral as they looked to me for guidance and answers. It was the hardest task I have ever been asked to take on.

On the front row close to where their father's body lay, sat his four young children. With tears in their eyes, I promised them that I would do all I could to be there for them and help them as they go through life, while knowing in the back of my mind the enormous challenges that lay ahead for them. Upon returning to class a week after the funeral, I once again sat in class, this time unfocused, nonresponsive, miserable, and anxious to leave. All I could think about was, if I was finding it difficult to focus and learn as an adult PhD student who had been traumatized, how must my little nieces and nephews feel?

Those fears were soon confirmed when I spoke to their mother and learned that they were now struggling in school. They did not just wake up and forget how to be good students, but they did wake up traumatized. Their mother shared with me how she has had to deal with the mood swings, nightmares, and confusion.

Now their trauma has begun to show up in their behavior at school and the disengagement and trouble has begun. But I argue that they are not the only ones disengaged at school. Much of their disengagement has stemmed from their teachers who expected them to snap back to normal even though their normal had changed. I honestly believe that their teachers somehow believed that because they were working with a population of kids that have historically experienced more trauma in the context of neighborhood violence, that they should be able to get over it more quickly because they are more used to it.

This denial of a young person's trauma and unwillingness to understand their cultural reality and pain is the number one reason so many kids are currently disengaging from school. It is ultimately why

I disengaged from school as a kid and why I felt compelled to write this book.

I write this book because I know what it feels like to not have my pain affirmed and acknowledged. I also know what it feels like to be isolated because of my race, gender, socio-economic class, learning style, and world-view. But most importantly, I write this book because I know what it feels like to be a lost kid out there in this cold world, walking around scared and scarred with a heavy heart, wondering if I will make it.

For every kid who has been forced to sit silently in class while your heart is crying out, this book is for you. And to my nephew Steven Hanley and the children you left behind, DShawn Trinity, Kyla and Lil Steven. I love you and you are the reason that I dedicate my life to helping others. Together we will make it.

R.I.P. "Nephew"
Steven D. Hanley

Introduction

What Does It Mean to be a Dis-Engaged Student?

My life was not easy as a kid in school. As a matter a fact, starting at an early age, it was school that made much of my life the nightmare that it was. As I have written about in my books *The Dropout, Wrestling for My Life and Me and my Homies*, my struggles and successes as a disengaged student extended far beyond the classroom, but were heavily influenced and preceded by my classroom experiences.

There was nothing lonelier then being misunderstood, miscommunicated with and ultimately mislabeled, by a teacher when I was just a child. I internalizing the notion that because I did not learn the way the teacher was trained to teach, that that somehow meant I was not capable of learning, or even worse, worthy of learning. This misunderstanding of who I was and how I felt often led to conflict and the resentment of my teachers, ultimately serving as the catalyst for me dropping out of school at the age of 17. But this was not before I had experienced a lifetime of let downs, setbacks, and disappointments at the hands of educators, and other outside forces.

It started with being mislabeled and placed in Special Education when I was a 3rd grader, after being a top student in 1st and 2nd grade. It was that nightmarish experience that broke my spirits almost to the point of no return. These events also set me on the course of writing this book. With that being said, I write this book with a heavy heart, as I am once again forced to relive these tumultuous times of my life, but I am also filled with joy as I ponder the possibilities in knowing that through my stories, struggles, observations and ideas young minds will be saved and children's lives will be enhanced.

It is not a coincidence that the better education a kid receives the less likely they are to end up in jail or wasting away out on the streets. But it is also no coincidence that the better a kid feels about his or her teacher the more productive they will be in the classroom. As educators we all know the disengaged student in our classrooms and the challenges that comes with teaching them. This book is an attempt to help us reexamine the widely agreed upon belief it's the kids that are the ones that are disengaged. We will go deeper and ask a different question: "Is it the kids that are disengaged, or is it educators and administrators/the system that is disengaged?" This question will be examined as it pertains to the realities in which many students are living and the approaches we as educators are taking.

Maybe it is time that we reimagine what engaging student looks like. Our students are dealing with real life problems, we often offer abstract solutions, and then we call them disengaged. One would have a great argument that it is the systems disengaged approach to education that is causing the disengagement. Much of my perspective has very little to do with academics but everything to do with relationship building, and how the academic approaches that were void of relationship failed me in the past as they are currently failing students today.

During this age when test scores are the barometer by which we measure student achievement, it is important that we not forget the most basic skill needed to teach a student. Trust. Before there can be learning there must be trust. It is through trust that we have had the greatest impact on students. This underrated quality, more than any other approach, has given many educators the space to engage students and inspire them to learn. It has also been the lack of trust that has contributed to many teachers not fully getting through to their students.

In order to truly touch our student's hearts, we must allow them to first feel our hearts. As with any healthy relationship, humility and vulnerability must be present. When these are present we create spaces for transformative learning to take place, and it is through these modes that we become better learners of our students while simultaneously becoming better teachers to them.

This is what it means to engage the Disengaged Student. It is my prayer and my hope that upon reading this book that you will find a story that connects with you, and can be applied to the way you view education and go about engaging your students.

Many of you have seen the great challenges that lie ahead of us and sometimes feel overwhelmed and as if you are not making a difference. I want you to know that every morning you wake up and travel to work to give your all you are making a difference in the lives of your students. Many kids are growing up in challenging communities and have had people in and out of their lives all of their lives, so for you to return when so many have left them, makes all the difference in the world. She/he will always remember you as I remember the ones who touched my heart and my life. As you have answered the call to educate our nation's children know that you are all truly heroes and agents of change.

1st Grade

Welcome to the Neighborhood

"It's not a neighborhood school if it's not a part of the neighborhood."

My mama loaded me and my brothers up on a one way Greyhound bus to leave the Texas farm where I was born after she and my dad got divorced. Gone were the open fields and fruit trees. Gone were the walks with my pole down to the creek to catch fish, and gone were all of the family members I was used to being surrounded by. My brothers and 1 were alone and life would never be the same, especially for me. No food, no furniture, and no extended family members to call my own. These are the most vivid memories of my early years In Oklahoma City.

What I remember most about those first years in Oklahoma City is that there were roaches everywhere and no food to eat in our small apartment. The crack epidemic was in its infancy, still brewing. We had no idea that the neighborhood we were living in is where the eye of the storm would soon touch down and produce massive gang and drug wars. Death, incarceration, and brokenness would soon grip the predominately black side of Oklahoma, City, better known as the Eastside. This was my new home, and for a country boy from an East Texas farm, living in the city felt like a whole new world.

Many days, my brothers and I spent every waking hour inside of our apartment killing roaches and experimenting with whatever edible thing we could turn into a meal. We did not know anyone in our new apartment complex the way we did back home in Texas, so we were anxious to make new friends.

Because my brothers were older they were allowed to leave the apartment when my mama was gone but I was not. Being the youngest, as usual, I found myself in what would become a very familiar place for me, a place called "by myself".

Because my brothers were older, they attended a different school than I, so once again I was alone. No kid has cried and suffered from separation anxiety more than I did on my first day at my new school. I remember my mom taking me into the office. A few moments later she walked me to my classroom, kissed me bye and attempted to walk away, but I would not let her go that easy. It took maybe an hour for her to pry me off of her legs because I ran after her every time she tried to leave. I wasn't feeling being left alone at a new school in this new city where I knew no one, and no one knew me.

After the final warning to let her go, I remember walking into my classroom with my head held down and tears flowing. Out of nowhere, I heard a sweet ladies voice say to me, "It's gone be okay baby, you're in good hands now, come give me a hug and take a seat". My new teacher was about 60 years old and had the biggest, warmest smile on her face. There was something about her that just made me feel like I was back at home and everything was going to be okay.

Every day when my mom and my classmates parents picked us up, my teacher did all she could to talk to all of the parents. But it was not the kind of talking that most teachers engage in with parents – talk that usually revolves around all things school and what trouble their kid got into for the day. She was more interested in our lives outside of school, especially mine. She genuinely wanted to know all about us and she also shared stories about herself and her family.

I vividly remember her always taking the time out to ask my mom how things were going and whether she needed anything. For many weeks I remember my mom always saying, "No, we are fine", but the truth is, we were not fine. At the time we didn't even have running water because of a past due bill. We never had all of our utilities on at the same time, nor was there enough food in our apartment for me and my brothers to have a full meal. My mom was doing all she could to make a way for us, but it was hard. Even as a little kid I could tell she was drowning.

The one thing I noticed about my teacher was that she listened to every word that people said to her and even had an amazing ability to hear words that had gone unspoken. She always seemed to really care about how others were doing. So, in many ways, it was no surprise that one month into the school year, she rolled out a large suitcase, and two large stapled bags. After school she said, "Now listen I gotta leave early today but you give these here bags to your mama when she picks you up, and tell her she will be in trouble with me if she doesn't take them". I wanted to look inside of them but I knew I would get into trouble myself, so I waited for my mom to arrive.

About 15 minutes later when she picked me up, I

remember watching her open the suit case and bags, and then break down crying, much like I had on my first day at this new school. But her tears were tears of joy. The suitcase was filled with clothes for me and my brothers and the bags were filled with food. That night we ate the best meal we had eaten since we left Texas and I had my best night of sleep.

The next day when my mom arrived at the school to pick me up she walked over to my teacher and thanked her. "You are so welcome," she said, "That's what family is for. You're Joseph's mother, but he's one of my babies, too. He can't learn like he needs to if he has no food to eat and feels bad about having to wear dirty clothes to school. Sugar, I'm from a time when folks in the community took care of each other and my teachers did the same for me. As a result my parents were willing to give my teachers whatever they needed. You see, it takes a village and I'm not just here to teach, I'm here to help you to raise Joseph into a fine young man. So y'all don't worry one bit. Just keep working hard like you're doing to raise them babies and everything is gonna be alright"

From that day on my mom was a fixture at the school, doing whatever she could to help out. Whenever she was called upon by my teacher she would show up ready to work, no questions asked. Yes, she was my teacher, but because of how she treated us, she was considered an extended family member and my mom was willing to do whatever she wanted her to do, not out of fear but out of respect and love

THINGS I WISH MY TEACHER KNEW

In this chapter I have nothing to say about the things that I wish my teacher knew about me, but rather the things that I felt I learned from her and her approach to education. From the day she told my mother, "I'm not just here to teach", I have never looked at the field of education the same. I understood what she meant when she said she came from a time when the community took care of one another and that she felt a sense of responsibility to help raise me. She was speaking of what a true community was and what a true community school looked like. She taught me that it is not enough to just have a school in an underserved community and not serve the needs of the kids and families of that community. She approached education as a servant first. Even though we had no food to eat and no lights in the house, she made me feel comfortable at school because she showed me that she cared. It was a simple approach. The more she served us the more comfortable she made us, and the more she made us comfortable, the more we were willing to do for her. This was only made possible by her engaging in constant communication with my mom, working to get to know her, and learning how she could best help our family. She did not help us because she was using us to get what she wanted; she helped us because she saw that we had a need and truly cared about us. I also believe that by her taking the time to engage us and go the extra mile, she was also building a deep level of trust with my family that was going to pay her back in a major way. My mom would have done anything for her because she knew that my teacher cared. In return she got the most out of me academically.

My teacher understood the demographics of the people she was serving and knew most of the parents in this particular area did not have a lot of education themselves. For many, the trauma and stigmatization from underachieving at school when they were children still haunted them. School was a very intimidating place to them, so they needed someone who made them feel comfortable in a place where there had been so much discomfort.

ENGAGEMENT APPROACH

First, let me make it clear, I am not saying that

teachers should start buying food and clothes for their students. My teacher had the means and made a decision to do so, and for that particular situation it turned out for the best. The truth is, even if she had not given us food and clothes, just her embracing my family and making me and my mom feel welcomed into the new school community was priceless. My teacher did not wait on a PTA meeting or parent teacher conferences to get to know my mom or my classmate's parents. She reached out and engaged with them every time she could, which made them feel welcomed. This is how a community school welcomed a new family during the time when schools were not just in a community but a part of the community. In return, if any problems or concerns arose, she had the trust of the parents which made it easier to have sometimes very difficult conversations with them, before things escalated. Because of this, everyone was informed and on the same page. This created an amazing and extremely healthy classroom culture where everyone felt like they mattered and were a part of a village.

As an educator how much time are you spending building a relationship with your students' parents? If you're not spending time, making a phone call during your break to just check in with parents is a great way to start. Correspond with them through social media, and talk with them every chance you get when they pick up their kids in the morning, evening and at school functions. A handshake, a hug, or a little conversation that is not always about education can go a long way in building parental trust and getting better student outcomes.

I know that many who are reading this are thinking, "All of this sounds great, but I just don't have time". As a former teacher, Dean of Students and now educational consultant I have experienced and witnessed the time crunch that teachers are under. I understand the frustration and stress that the limited time produces, but as educators we must be real with ourselves as we come to terms with the reality that a lack of time due to school structure and facing the social challenges of our students is, unfortunately, just a part of teaching.

Given this reality we must now ask ourselves the real questions "What do we want to spend our time doing? What is the best way to get the job done?" Because the reality is, the time will be spent either way. We will either spend it proactively speaking to our students' parents before they get into trouble, or we will spend it reactively sitting in conferences after our kids have acted out and disrupted our whole class. We will either spend time on the front end talking to our students' parents, discovering more about their lives and how we as a collective village can best help our children learn, or we will spend the time on the back end talking to them about why their kids grades are so low, as we try to figure out why they never have their homework done, seem to not care much for school, and miss a lot of days. As educators we will either spend proactive time on the front end asking our students' parents about how their children learn at home or on the reactive back end in our Principal/Head of School offices answering questions during evaluation time about why the kids are not learning in the classroom. There is no getting around the fact that the time will be spent, we just have to ask ourselves how and where we want to spend that time.

As an educator, I have heard other educators express the sentiment that they don't need or cannot reach parents because they don't care about their kids' education. As I will expand on in a later chapter, I also heard that being said about my mom when I was a young student. I am asking my fellow educators not to buy into the negative narratives about parents, because if we do then we help to push parents away and create an 'us versus them' culture instead of a community.

I recognize that the current fast pace of education with the rigid outlines, outcomes, and expectations do not allow a lot of space for true relationship building with our students' families and communities, but this reality does not wipe away the fact that though policies and practices continue to change, people's basic need to be loved, connected, respected, embraced and appreciated do not. Just as we as educators feel that having support in all of these basic needs in our work environment helps us better teach our students, we must understand that parents have many similar basic needs, and when they are met by their children's teacher and school they become our greatest allies in the education of the kids in the village.

IN SUMMARY

A 2009 study by Nzinga-Johnson et al. found that a parent-teacher relationship characterized by warmth, trust, and communication is one of the most important predictors of parent involvement. Other studies have shown that healthy parent-teacher relationships improve student achievement, increase parent involvement, and improve early school adjustment (Fan & Chen, 2001; Henderson & Mapp, 2002; Marcon, 1999; Reynolds, 1991). There is also evidence that poor parent-teacher relationships are associated with lower student achievement trajectories for African American students in early grades (Hughes, et al. 2007). My first grade teacher knew this, and she worked to foster warm, trusting relationships with parents with the goal of ensuring that every child in her care received the best education possible. A true community school that embraces families can make all the difference in how parents engage in their child's education. Most parents want what is best for their children and care deeply about their education. Teachers can play a major role in maximizing parent involvement and student potential by understanding that:

✐ You cannot fully educate students without embracing parents;

✐ You must have sensitivity to and understanding

of the cultural and socioeconomic realities of students in order to have a true understanding of how to provide the best education experience possible.

When students' basic needs are not met it is difficult for them to focus on their education. Helping families to access resources can go a long way in improving the educational experience of the entire family.

REFERENCES

1. Fan, X., & Chen, M. (2001). Parental involvement and students' academic achievement: A meta-analysis. *Educational Psychology Review*, 13, 1–22.

2. Henderson, A. T., & Mapp, K. L. (2002). A new wave of evidence: The impact of school, family, and community connections on student achievement. Annual Synthesis 2002. Austin, TX: Southwest Educational Development Laboratory,

National Center for Family & Community Connections with Schools. Available from www.sedl.org/ connections/resources/evidence.pdf

3. Hughes, J., & Kwok, O. M. (2007). Influence of student-teacher and parent-teacher relationships on lower achieving readers' engagement and achievement in the primary grades. *Journal of Educational Psychology*, 99(1), 39.

4. Marcon, R. A. (1999). Positive relationships between parent school involvement and public inner-city preschoolers' development and academic performance. *School Psychology Review*, 28, 395–412.

5. Nzinga-Johnson, S., Baker, J. A., & Aupperlee, J. (2009). Teacher-Parent Relationships and School Involvement among Racially and Educationally Diverse Parents of Kindergartners. *The Elementary School Journal*, 110(1), 81-91.

2nd Grade

Affirmation

"The greatest gift that you can give a kid is to affirm the gift that they have."

By the time 2nd grade rolled around I had moved away from the school where my first grade teacher taught. My mom truly wanted me to stay there, but after we were evicted from our apartment she had no choice but to take me out. My new school was a few miles away and still in the same district, so once again I had to make new friends and get to know a new teacher all over again.

The one thing that my 2nd grade teacher and I

learned about me really quick is that I hated sitting down in one place for long periods of time and was willing to do whatever I could to get the chance to move around. I also hated long periods of reading and quiet times. At first I tried to sit still for a long time and focus on my work like the rest of the kids, but I was unable to. There was just something inside of me that took me away. Most of the time it was a song, not just a song that I had heard on the radio, but rather, a song that I had created in my mind. My body just wanted to dance to the melody. What seemed like a few moments of checking out to me would usually end with my teacher having to snap me out of my dream state and tell me what I missed.

My 2nd grade teacher was a young, short, red haired white lady who looked like peppermint patty from Charlie Brown. She was really good at engaging my imagination. "Joseph! Joseph! Joseph!" After the third time of her calling my name I usually snapped out of the song world that I was visiting and every time she got me out of my dream state she always asked me what I was thinking. That was something that my mom did frequently. After I answered she always found a way to make the lesson come to life, and more relevant by tying whatever my song or day dream was about to the work we were doing for the day. She always made me feel like she truly cared about my dreams and how I felt about things. She also made it a point to give me the greatest incentives in the world. After she realized that I was a creative fireball she became more understanding and came up with a plan that she and I could agree on.

My teacher started to notice that the biggest challenge for me was not the classwork that we were doing. It was considered rigorous, but for me it wasn't. Although I saw many of my classmates struggle to get their assignments done correctly, I just seemed to get it. I often completed my work much faster than everyone else, so I when I finished I would just check out until it was time for the next subject. This served as a major source of boredom and restlessness. She noticed that these were usually the main times that I would slip into my musical dream state. Instead of punishing me by making me suppress what I was feeling or making me feel like I was an outcast, one day she said, "Joseph, I don't mind you thinking about music, but I don't want you to just think about it, I want you to write about it. But first I need you to do something for me. If you finish your assignments and everything is correct, I will let you go stand up in the back of the room and write your songs and thoughts as long as you do it quietly." From that day on I finished my work early just so I could get all of the thoughts and music out of my head.

One day I finished early and she asked me if I wanted to be her helper, which would require me to walk around and help my classmates. Excitedly I said, "Like a teacher?" "Yes, like a teacher," she said, "and maybe you can even write a song or rap about the work and recite it for the class. That day, Joseph the teacher was born. Math, reading, science it did not matter the subject, I was just so happy to have the opportunity to answer questions and walk around to help my classmates. There was nothing more rewarding than helping someone, and hearing another student call my name to come over and help them. It made me feel really useful and important. She became my favorite teacher and it was apparent that I was her favorite student.

The highlight of being the teacher's helper was when she allowed me to teach my own English lesson. She gave me free reign to use poetry, rap, and act out my lesson. It was the greatest experience I had been a part of in my young academic life. To see every kid in the classroom paying attention to me and following my directions was a foreshadowing of what my life was supposed to be. I had always been a leader and had the desire to lead others. I just needed the opportunity to do so in a way that was most comfortable for me. Allowing me to teach class through the arts was a great foundation for me to learn how to have a positive impact on the classroom instead of a negative one. The alternative – suppressing my energy and creativity – would have resulted in me rebelling against her attempt to force me into becoming the stereotypical model of a "good student". Instead, she recognized who I was and that I was already a "good student", and that my learning style brought diversity to the classroom.

THINGS I WISH MY TEACHER KNEW

I wish she would have known that my learning style would probably not be embraced by other teachers and in traditional learning environments.

Although my teacher understood my learning style, many other less patient and creative teachers that I later encountered did not. I only had one year with her so once the year was over I moved on. The odds were slim that I would have another teacher like her.

Perhaps she could have reached out to or written a letter for the teacher whose classroom I would be in the next year but that never happened.

I wish she would have known that I could have benefitted from being tested for the Gifted and Talented program.

I believe that if tested I would have been placed in the program talented and gifted program. No matter where I moved I would have at least had a record following me, showing that I had the capacity to be a high achiever.

I wish she would have communicated with school administrators about how her differentiated teaching style benefitted all of the children in the classroom.

I recall one day the principal walked into our classroom and questioned her about me standing up writing in the back of class. I always wondered what she would tell him because he never stayed for a very long. It turns out that she was under a lot of pressure for stepping out of the box to engage me. If I could go back I would have asked her to invite him in to watch her teach and see how she effectively differentiated her teaching style/ instruction for the diverse learners in the classroom, and the results that it produced. Maybe if she had been more outgoing and showed the principal that there were other methods of educating and engaging students other than the way they wanted her to teach, she would have not been considered a bad teacher but rather a creative one. Towards the end of the year I found out that they were not happy with her approach. I overheard a conversation she had with another teacher from down the hall telling her that her contract was not being renewed the next year.

ENGAGEMENT APPROACH

At a time when teachers are under unprecedented

pressure to use prescriptive teaching and pedagogical approaches, it is difficult to figure out how to follow the script while simultaneously incorporating creative and artistic approaches in the classroom and meeting the needs of our diverse learners. Teachers are being forced to balance preparing their students for high stakes tests while fighting to maintain creative and curricular control (Darling-Hammond, 1999; Gipps, 1999). In this environment, repetition, drilling, and rote memorization have become a part of many classrooms today, even though higher order skills such as critical thinking and creative thinking are often suppressed by these methods ((Deci, Kasser & Ryan, 1997; Hattie, Jaeger & Bond, 1999). Extensive research demonstrates that working to incorporate the arts and creative approaches in our classrooms is well worth the fight (Darby and Catterall, 1994; Oreck, 2006; Lynch 2007).

As we glance through the landscape of pop culture today we see that more than any other form of entertainment, music is the most powerful force on the planet. The influence that many musical artists have over others is undeniable. They shape the way millions of people think, speak, and dress and in many ways act and dream. As a performing artist myself, I use multiple art forms to reach and teach students, but it is through the power of music that I have seen people moved the most. Although I believe I have an amazing gift of storytelling and jumping into different characters to "edutain" (educate + entertain) the crowd, it is through my music that I take them to the next level. I do this because of my firsthand experience of how a teacher used the arts to engage me.

Let me make it clear, I am not saying that a teacher should rap, sing and act for their students. Rather, I am suggesting that we explore how we can incorporate those mediums into our classrooms. Students writing raps about the findings and perspectives that they have come up with in the classroom is one approach. Educational expressions that are inspired by their outside surroundings is a way to make school work come to life for many students (Morrell & Duncan-Andrade, 2002; Stovall, 2006). The use of hip hop in classrooms is a growing trend that I hope continues, but it is not enough for them to just listen to others voices. They must be allowed to find and develop their own voice. This can come through the spoken word, raps, poetry, monologues or providing them the opportunity to feel what it is like to prepare a lesson and teach a class, the way my teacher did.

We are all leaders in some capacity. Some of us are leaders when it comes to being an example of what it means to sit down and be quiet and attentive. Those are the kind of leaders that most teachers love as they allow them to teach without any interruptions. These kids are the ones who are most likely to get pegged and developed as leaders mainly because of how comfortable they make teachers feel. They give them very little push back and cause them no disruptions. These kinds of students are typically viewed in a more positive light. As an educator I have had students like this. I have thoroughly enjoyed the peace and harmony that they bring to the classroom. But I also have an appreciation of kids who are leaders like I was. These students are not going to allow the teacher to just teach without them being intimately involved and personally engaged. In other words, it's alright for there to be a little learning noise brought by the hyperactive kids, too. In my opinion, they bring the excitement, creativity and healthy tension that help to foster dialogue. Unfortunately, because of society's view of what it means to be a leader and good student, kids with this personality type tend to be considered "problem kids" as they are so far on the other end of the spectrum of what a "good student" is.

As we assess or classroom culture, we must ask ourselves if we create safe spaces for all of our students to lead. We must make sure that we are not only rewarding the ones who say very little, or the outgoing ones who must be seen, and snuggle up to us.

But, do we create spaces for the kids who are a little more challenging, distant and not considered conventional learners or good students? Do we create safe spaces for the students who are overly talkative and active or the class clowns? These children tend to be some of the strongest leaders in classroom settings, but also tend to get into the most trouble. A lot of the reason they get into trouble is because they have no safe place to share their unique gifts so they are forced to suppress them and eventually this becomes their and our classrooms undoing.

IN SUMMARY

Through the arts every child in our classroom has an opportunity to lead and shine. It seems like the use of music and the arts to connect with students gets put on the back burner or completely abandoned after around second grade. This is unfortunate because the love of music and the arts remains in our hearts forever. I have always observed that students respond to creative classroom cultures. I think it is important not to forget how much we loved the arts growing up. We must remember how we learned how to talk, how to play and how to think through the arts. This was our experience, and it worked wonders for our learning experiences in school. So it is imperative that we now question any approach to education that does not allow room for us to use the arts or discourages us from using them to engage our students.

REFERENCES

1. Darby, J., & Catterall, J. (1994). The fourth R: The arts and learning. *The Teachers College Record*, *96*(2), 299-328.

2. Darling-Hammond, L. (Ed.) (1999). *Teaching as the Learning Profession: Handbook of Policy and Practice.* San Francisco: Jossey Bass.

3. Deci, E.L., Kasser, T., & Ryan, R.M. (1997). Self-

determined teaching: opportunities and obstacles. In J. L. Bess (Ed.). *Teaching well and liking it: Motivating faculty to teach effectively* (pp. 57-71). Baltimore: Johns Hopkins.

4. McCullar, C.K. (1998). *Integrated curriculum: An approach to collegiate preservice teacher training using the fine arts in the elementary classroom* (Doctoral dissertation, Texas Tech University).

5. Gipps, C. (1999). Socio-cultural aspects of assessment. In A. Iran-Nejad & P.D. Pearson (Eds.). *Review of Research in Education*, 24, 355-392. Washington, DC: American Education Research Association.

6. Hattie, J., Jaeger, R.M., & Bond, L. (1999). Persistent methodological questions in educational testing. In A. Iran-Nejad & P.D. Pearson (Eds.). *Review of Research in Education*, 24, 393-446. Washington, DC: American Education Research Association.

7. Lynch, P. (2007). Making Meaning Many Ways: An Exploratory Look at Integrating the Arts with Classroom Curriculum. *Art Education, 60*(4), 33-38.

8. Morrell, E., & Duncan-Andrade, J. M. (2002). Promoting academic literacy with urban youth through engaging hip-hop culture. *English Journal*, 88-92.

9. Oreck, B. (2006). Artistic choices: A study of teachers who use the arts in the classroom. *International Journal of Education & the Arts*, 7(8), 1-27.

10. Stovall, D. (2006). We can relate hip-hop culture, critical pedagogy, and the secondary classroom. *Urban Education, 41*(6), 585-602.

3ʳᵈ Grade

Not so Special

"Don't clip my wings and then punish me because I cannot fly."

Starting out, I was by no means a troubled or angry kid. It was not until I entered this particular school and began being punished for my desire to hold on to who I was, that the troubles began. From the time I was born, music and creative expression was my life. I was being brought up by a mother who was an artist and always dreamed of moving to New York to become an actress and singer. It was the most fun childhood that a kid could have imagined. Although we often had no money and little food, we always had a lot of love and arts going on in our home. My childhood memories are filled with my mama singing me to sleep and waking me up to song. Because I am the youngest of six boys, my childhood memories are also full of memories that involved nightly fights, wrestling matches and proving that we were the toughest brothers in our neighborhood. But because of my mom we were also the most artistic and sensitive kids around.

The highlight of my week was always when my brothers and I came together for what we called "Family Talent Night". One by one we stood up and told jokes, sang, danced, rapped, acted, and laughed together. This was the only world that I knew and I loved it. It was a safe space where I felt unconditionally loved and accepted for who I was. My 1st and 2nd grade teachers understood me and created the environment for me to be successful by allowing me to use the gifts that I possessed. I didn't I know my life was about to be turned upside down when I entered 3rd grade. I was about to enter a new world called the "other side of town", better known as the suburbs.

I can still remember my first day of 3rd grade and the culture shock that ensued upon entering my new school. The word was that this school district had the best schools around. Because my mom wanted to provide what was best for her kids, she found a new place for us to live so we could attend a "better school".

As we all know, parents are our first teachers. My mother and first teacher was great. She understood how I learned and created a nurturing environment for me to do so. She was very in tune with me and as a result I was in tune with what she wanted to teach me. I watched her make up songs and act out different scenarios to teach me and my brothers. But she also allowed us to creatively respond back to her. Our home was a classroom and this classroom was hands on and interactive. Above all, it inspired us to learn.

I thought my new school classroom would be like the one I had at home, and the others I had been a part of in first and second grade. I thought it would be like one big family, like an extension of the one that I came from. But I was wrong. It was the complete opposite. On the first day of school, my new teacher sternly instructed the students to "sit down in this assigned seat, in this assigned row, be quiet, look straight ahead, walk in this straight line, and color inside this line". When I did not comply with all of the rules I was accused of being out of line. It didn't take long for the trouble to begin. I quickly started thinking there was something wrong with school and something wrong with me.

Every day as the music played during writing time, I quietly recited the songs and raps I wrote about the book I chose to read. My teacher always made it a point to stop my flow and make me write the way the other kids were writing. It was not that I had a problem writing my classroom assignments how she wanted me to; it was that I would see the text through a creative lens and wanted to give a creative and critical response. She wanted me to just summarize, like the rest of my classmates.

When she asked us a question I always heard musical answers and wanted to jump up and act the scenario out to come up with the answer, like I did at home with my family and in my other schools. But this practice of creative expression was always met with resistance as I was constantly asked to sit down or go to time out. As a result, I started becoming disengaged in school. I eventually became angry because I felt like the teacher was denying my freedom. Further, I watched my peers academically pull ahead. Most of them were not as creative or expressive as I was, nor were they smarter, but they succeeded because they never attempted to push her to differentiate her instruction.

Her pressure to suppress my free spirit ignited an educational wildfire around me that continued to burn me throughout my years in school. The more she pushed to keep me quiet, the angrier and more disruptive I became. The more disruptive I became, the more trouble I got into. This trouble took me away from instruction time and caused me to fall even further behind. I was in a vicious cycle that I was unable to get out of.

What does a kid do when his or her way of life is under attack? What does a kid do when his/her natural rhythm is interrupted and their free spirited wings are violently clipped? For some kids, the response to having their creativity suppressed is to conform, but just not give their all. They give just enough to get by and be left alone. My instinct was to rebel against whatever I felt was hurting me.

The behavior that I displayed once my teacher started shutting down my creativity was nothing more than an act of survival, a desire to breath. My teacher and other school administrators saw it as a disinterest in school and an act of defiance or "oppositional defiance" as they called it. I just wanted to be engaged and allowed to be myself, but as the weeks went by, the spark that I had for learning began to dim and leave my spirited soul. I was rarely called on to answer questions, so I would blurt the answers out. She knew that I liked to give longer answers where I drew from different life experiences and acted the question out to make my point. I also followed up her questions to the students with a question for her. She hated this because it required her to become a student for a moment and she always loved hearing herself talk and staying on her tight, rigid schedule.

I vividly remember thinking, "she just doesn't like me", because based on my life experiences, people who cared for one another, listened to one another, respected each other's point of view and demonstrated curiosity, vulnerability and humility when they encountered something that they did not understand. As her discomfort with my learning style became more apparent my young life spiraled out of control right in front of her but she never once attempted to catch me. The more I spiraled downward, the more depressed I became, and the less effort I gave in class. And then it happened…

Six weeks into the school year I was informed that I was being moved to a new classroom. At first I was excited. I would do anything to get out of this teachers class, until I found out that my new classroom was Special Education. This journey into Special Education was and still is the worst experience of my school life. I cannot remember a time that I have cried more. I just wanted someone to rescue me from that classroom, but no one ever came. They said it was for my own good, but in my heart I knew it was punishment for being different and having a different learning style. I was being punished because she was unable to teach me.

While in her class I began acting out because I felt restricted in the classroom structure and I was bored to death by the lack of creativity and rigorous work I was being asked to do, without the freedom to use my gifts.

As my punishment I was placed in an even more restrictive and confining space where the work was twice as easy and the pace was twice as slow. For my teacher, it was great because I was out of her hair; however, as far as I was concerned, nothing good came out of them placing me in Special Education. Although the many tears I shed in that classroom eventually dried up, the trauma and stigmatization lasted a lifetime. To this day that experience is a major contributor to the PTSD (Post Traumatic School Disorder) that I carry with me every day.

THINGS I WISH MY TEACHER KNEW

The wide range of individual differences surely must mean that there is no single method for nurturing creativity; ideally, the experiences we provide should be tailor-made, if not for individual students, at least for different types of students. We should remember that the same fire that melts the butter hardens the egg.

(MacKinnon, 1978, p. 171)

According to research, educational settings that foster creativity should include time for creative thinking, rewards for creative ideas and outputs, allowing room for mistakes, imagining and embracing other viewpoints, and questioning assumptions, generating multiple hypotheses, and focusing on broad ideas rather than specific facts. (Sternberg & Williams, 1996); Starko, 2013). I would have benefitted from and thrived in this type of learning environment and many of our students could benefit from such and environment. The things I wish my 3rd grade teacher knew about me are centered on recognizing and appreciating my creativity and finding ways to allow all of her students to be more free and creative in the classroom.

I wish my teacher understood that what and how I learned at home was an asset to the classroom and

not a liability.

Every student is unique, and by discovering the talents and gifts and learning how to allow each student to express those talents and gifts, we as teachers can enrich our teaching experience, enhance the learning environment, and have healthier, happier students. The book *Structure and Improvisation in Creative Teaching* (Sawyer, 2011) states that "effective creative teaching strikes a delicate balance between structure and improvisation". This is an important lesson for every educator. It takes creativity to harness and channel the creative expression of their students. My second grade teacher found effective strategies for getting me to complete the required assignments while still allowing me to be myself. She used allowing me to be creative in the classroom as an incentive to complete classwork and comply with classroom rules. She understood that by striking this balance, she was nurturing my love for learning and developing my creativity.

I wish my teacher had taken time to reach out to my mom to find out more about my home life and my learning style.

Research indicates that when schools, families and community stakeholders work together, achievement gaps decrease (Epstein & Van Voorhis, 2010; Henderson & Mapp, 2002; Holcomb-McCoy, 2010). As I discussed above, my home environment played a big role in my creativity. If my teacher had established a partnership with my mother and had asked her questions about why I was the way I was, she might have understood me better. She may have gotten a clearer picture of why I used music and improvisation to learn and remember new material. I wish she understood that my desire to rhythmically express myself derived from a deeply embedded instinct and a cultural upbringing at home where I was encouraged to move and play. If she had seen my mother as a valuable and viable partner in my education, my experience may have been much different, as I likely would have never ended up in Special Education.

ENGAGEMENT APPROACH

What if my teacher had called and spoke with my mom about how we engage and interact at home? How much more would she have found out about me and how I learned? Rather than sending me to a SPED class without testing me, she could have started by talking to previous teachers and having a discussion with my mother. What if she had recognized my creativity as promise and tested or recommended me for the talented and gifted program? I believe that there is a thin line between many kids who end up in talented and gifted classrooms and kids who end up in SPED. In my case, my talents and gifts were perceived as symptoms of a learning disability. I was later labeled as oppositional defiant because of the pent up anger from being mislabeled and what I felt was mistreatment.

If my third grade teacher had asked questions and corresponded with my previous teachers to receive more information about my learning style and behaviors as well as my home and classroom challenges, I think she would have seen me differently. Even if a kid is coming from another school I think it is important for us to learn more about the students coming into our classrooms before they arrive if possible. I have heard people say it is best not to know so you can be less influenced by the opinions of others. As competitive as most businesses are, you will find that the most successful and productive ones actually exchange ideas with each other. Yes they are still competitors and face down challengers everyday but ultimately, to accomplish their ultimate goal, they engage in the sharing of ideas and approaches to grow and better serve their customers.

Many of our schools share ideas on things like best practices and other great educational approaches, but when it comes to transferring information on how to best engage a student from a teacher to teacher perspective we have a long way to go. I am not saying that teachers who do not do this are not doing their job. From my experience I believe many would be doing just that, if given the time. It is my hope that more will find a way to be more informed about our future students learning styles as well as the previous teacher's instruction style, By doing so, they will be better prepared to serve our students instead of trying to figure it out on their own, or asking questions after the kids have fallen way behind and are now being disruptive.

IN SUMMARY

A 2005 study by Aljughaiman and Mowrer-Reynolds found that while most teachers reported having positive attitudes about creativity in the classroom, when surveyed, teachers had negative reactions to behaviors most often displayed by creative students. Teachers often perceive the behaviors of creative students, which include being playful, emotional, stubborn, and thinking critically (Torrance, 1963) as being disruptive and not conducive to completing assignments and meeting academic obligations. This conflict must be resolved in the classroom in order to maximize the learning of all students.

The importance of providing creative learning opportunities and allowing students to express themselves creatively in the classroom is established (Cole, Sugioka, & Lynch, 1999; Torrance, 1976). According to Amabile (1989), pressure to conform and rote learning can destroy creativity in school. When teachers encounter students with drastically different learning styles in their classrooms it can be a challenge to figure out how to integrate that student into the learning environment, but it is crucial that they do so. Teachers can begin by:

- Identifying students who seem to have unique learning styles and finding ways to creatively incorporate, rather than discourage their approaches to learning.

- Avoid making assumptions about students who seem disruptive or non-compliant. Spend time talking to parents and former teachers to develop strategies that will better engage them.

- Create a stimulating learning environment that encourages all students to express and demonstrate their talents, gifts, and abilities.

REFERENCES

1. Aljughaiman, A., & Mowrer-Reynolds, E. (2005). Teachers' conceptions of creativity and creative students. The Journal of Creative Behavior, 39(1), 17-34.

2. Amabile, T. M. (1989). Growing up creative. Buffalo, NY: The Creative Education Foundation.

3. Cole, D., Sugioka, H., & Yamagata-Lynch, L. (1999). Supportive classroom environments for creativity in higher education. Journal of Creative Behavior, 33(4), 277-93.

4. de Souza Fleith, D. (2000). Teacher and student perceptions of creativity in the classroom environment. Roeper Review, 22(3), 148-153.

5. Epstein, J. L. (1995). School/family/community partnerships: Caring for the children we share. Phi delta kappan, 76(9), 701.

6. Epstein, J. L., & Van Voorhis, F. L. (2010). School counselors' roles in developing partnerships with families and communities for student success. Professional School Counseling, 14, 1–14.

7. Henderson, A. T., & Mapp, K. L. (Eds.). (2002). A new wave of evidence: The impact of school, family, and community connections on student achievement. Austin, TX: National Center for Family and Community Connections With Schools, Southwest Educational Development Laboratory.

Retrieved

from http://www.sedl.org/connections/research-syntheses.html.

8. Holcomb-McCoy, C. (2010). Involving low-income parents and parents of color in college readiness activities: An exploratory study. Professional School Counseling, 14, 115–124.

9. MacKinnon, D. W. (1978). In search of human effectiveness. Creative Education Foundation.

10. Sawyer, R. K. (Ed.). (2011). Structure and improvisation in creative teaching. Cambridge University Press.

11. Starko, A. J. (2013). *Creativity in the classroom: Schools of curious delight*. Routledge.

12. Sternberg, R. J., & Williams, W. M. (1996). How to develop student creativity. ASCD.

13. Torrance, E. P. (1963). The creative personality and the ideal pupil. Teachers College Record, 65, 220-226.

14. Torrance, E. P., & Safter, H. T. (1986). Are

children becoming more creative? The Journal of Creative Behavior, 20(1), 1-13.

Grade

Back to my Future

"You cannot prepare me for the future if you're always punishing me for my past."

For the rest of my time attending the school I entered in third grade, I was more disengaged than I had ever been in a school setting. Gone was the excitement and enthusiasm. Gone was the desire to work as hard as I could. Gone was the love and respect for "my teacher". She was now on my "watch list" a.k.a., my "untrustworthy list". I was angry, which led to the fights, trouble, and eventual suspensions. For many, this confirmed the "angry" label that I had been given.

Like many kids my age, I woke up for the first day of the new school year with the enthusiasm on my face matched only by the excitement of Christmas morning. At a very young age I was always aware of what a new beginning meant. New beginnings were something I had experienced all of my life because of the excessive amount of times my family moved. According to my mother, we moved 27 times in 8 years to be exact. This meant that in elementary I changed schools 2 to 3 times a year. I truly hated having to change schools, but I understood that when we could no longer pay our rent, it was time to go. The silver lining of moving so much was that it was an opportunity to have a new start. I was always hopeful that I would find a school that truly embraced my cultural and learning differences. Most of the time this was not the case. What usually waited for me were loneliness and isolation as I sat amongst my classmates being one of the only black kids in my school.

In a state like Oklahoma where African Americans are few in number, I found out what racism was at a very young age. Honestly, I don't know which nickname given to me by my classmates hurt more, "Nigger" or "Stupid Dummy". Though I often got into fights when I was called a nigger, I could depersonalize it and rationalize it as them just being ignorant and talking about all black people. On the other hand, being called a stupid dummy was very personal. I always took that taunt very hard. Secretly I cried about it when no one was around because I knew it wasn't true, but the environment was not allowing me to show my true self. With all I endured, to have the opportunity to return to the same school after summer break was a big deal for me. I really thought that this meant I would no longer be the "new kid" like I was used to being and would no longer be picked on.

The upcoming year was also especially big for me

because I had spent the entire summer down in East Texas reconnecting with my biological father who I had not seen in years and desperately wanted a relationship with. All summer long I woke up early in the morning and worked on my grandfather's farm, planting seeds, fishing, chasing chickens, helping my dad chop down trees, and loading them on to his truck. I also rode with him every day as he visited sick people and served the community as the town pastor. Engaging in these activities deeply impacted my life. I honestly believe the sense of belonging and connection that I had been craving and finally received from my father was the missing component of the happiness I was searching for.

I can only explain the feelings of my inner growth over that summer as a feeling of having grown taller. I felt like I had a new lease on life. I was finally being viewed in a positive light and given responsibilities, indicating that someone believed in me. This helped to facilitate my tremendous personal growth. Though I was not perfect by any means, I had calmed down a lot from being as impulsive as I had been in the past. There is something about giving a hyperactive child like myself responsibilities and positive reinforcements. This was truly the way to my heart and the fuel that I needed to propel me to the next level of my forever moving, thinking self.

I felt a sense of evolution when I came back to Oklahoma City from Texas. I did not recognize that even though I wanted to be better and to do better, this would not necessarily translate into being treated better. The previous year, I had been labeled a problem child who was "angry" by the teachers at the school, but somehow, I knew in my heart that this year was going to be different because I was determined to be a better student and person. On the morning of my first day of school as a new fourth grader, I woke with a fresh new outlook on life. I wanted to let go of the pain from the past and look forward to the future. As I was about to find out, it was not going to be so easy. I had no idea that I was already on the "watch list" aka "untrustworthy list".

After entering the classroom my new teacher told us all to find our assigned seats. One by one, my classmates found their desks and took a seat. Before I knew it, I was the last kid standing up still looking for my name. Then my teacher said, "Joseph, your seat is right here". To my disgust, she pointed to a desk that was separated from the rest of the class, the one that was right up front beside her desk. Not even 20 minutes into the school year and I was being singled out and placed in the spot that everyone knew was designated for the kids who always get into trouble.

Words cannot express the pain, anger and humiliation I felt as I sat down listened to my classmates snicker behind me. I must have gotten at least ten spit balls spat at the back of my head. Every time I turned around to see who was doing it my classmates would tell the teacher that I was turned around and she would chastise me for doing so. She never reprimanded the kids who were spitting paper at the back of my head.

I felt like a fool on display for the entertainment of others. It was bad enough that the previous year I had been the focal point of many of my classmates', jokes which resulted in many fights that I never started but always finished. This was just one more thing that would make me stand out, as if being the only "poor, black kid" in class wasn't enough. I couldn't even look back, talk to, or interact with my classmates. It was as if I was in the classroom by myself. I was isolated, like I was in solitary confinement.

When we went to lunch and recess it was as if she was watching and waiting for me to get into trouble. When other kids laughed in class they were being funny. When I laughed I was being disruptive. When the other kids talked to me in class she would ask them to please be quiet. When I talked back to them I was told to go to the office or forced to miss recess.

After a few days of seeing how things were going, I

decided to ask her why I was being placed by her desk when I had done nothing wrong, and why I was always the one getting in trouble when the other kids were doing the same things? Her reply was cold and let me know that she thought she already knew everything she needed to know about me. She said, "I have already been told about you and all the problems you caused last year. If you think you're going to come into my classroom and be disruptive you are mistaken". I tried to defend myself and tell her that I was not the same person I was last year. And that this was a new year and I was a new person. She responded, "You could have fooled me. It has only been a few days into school and you have already been into trouble several times. You're just a trouble making kid and I'm going to make sure you are held responsible for your actions."

To be told that I was a trouble maker the first week of school let me know exactly where I stood with her. In my mind I knew that no matter what I did it was going to be seen through a negative lens because she had already made up her mind about me. So out of anger, for the rest of that semester I was as disruptive as I could be. This was the only way I felt I could get back at her and regain control of my life.

THINGS I WISH MY TEACHER KNEW

I wish that my teacher understood that you cannot prepare someone for the future if you're still punishing and penalizing them for mistakes made in the past.

In my teachers eyes I was guilty of something and she would not allow me to have a clean slate or the space to prove myself. As a result, I stopped engaging in her class and became extremely defiant towards her instruction. I felt very mistreated. This feeling produced mistrust, which produced resentment and a rebellious response. From the moment my teacher made it clear that I would not be given the opportunity to be a better person and student, I acted out in her class. I was doing this as a response to the energy she was giving me. Once I realized I was on her watch list, and she shot down my attempt to talk to her, I no longer trusted her. She became no different than the neighborhood police who harassed me. Actually, she was worse than them because although I had been harassed quite often by the police, the run-ins of abuse would usually last about 10 to 20 minutes and then I'd be on my way. At school, I was force to be with the teacher who I saw as my abuser 8 hours a day, 5 days a week. Who wouldn't be angry?

ENGAGEMENT APPROACH

As you reflect on this chapter I ask you to think about possible approaches that my teacher could have taken to engage me in the learning process. Ask yourself, "How would I respond if I knew that a "Non IEP" student entering my classroom had been a challenging student and had often been in trouble the year before?"

Though there are many approaches that can be taken in that situation it is important that we are aware of what works for our individual skill sets and approaches to education. It is no secret that great classroom management skills are the number one predictor of how successful a teacher will be. No matter how much you know or how great the lesson plan is, you will never be able to fully teach your students if there is chaos in the classroom. Just like we should have differentiated approaches for our students with varied learning styles we should also differentiate our approaches to classroom management. Classroom management is where it all starts and often times where it all fall apart. Just like there are IEPs for kids in SPED we should also have Individual Student Behavior i.e. success plans for our most challenging students.

What if on the first day of school when I walked in,

instead of her placing me by her desk, she sat down with me and developed a "Personalized Student Success Plan". This could have been something as simple as placing a board or piece of paper in a special spot somewhere on the wall in the room that reflects the time we spent talking. We could have discussed how I felt about my previous experiences, and areas where she and I felt I needed to improve. This plan could have spelled out what we needed from each other for the school year to go smoothly and differently than the previous one. If she had done this with me she could have also found out about the life changing summer experience I had in Texas with my dad.

Imagine if she would have had a conversation with him or my mom before I even entered into the classroom. She would have found out just how much I had grown and how hopeful I was for the new school year. This would have allowed her to build on the momentum from that trip, further creating a synergy between us. Instead of a "me against her" atmosphere it would have been more like a partnership where collectively, we could reflect on what we said we needed from each other and ourselves for my growth as well as hers.

I know the limited time that every single teacher in America is working with, and it is legitimate to look at the limited instruction and preparation time we have to do are jobs. Given these constraints it can often feel like we don't have the time to focus on a few individual kids; however, if we know the kids who have caused other teachers problems in the past it would probably be advantageous to give them the extra time and attention they need, because in the end they will get our attention for another reason. When that happens we will be doing very little teaching and the rest of our students will be doing very little learning.

IN SUMMARY

Educational research has found that as it relates to teaching and engaging boys in classroom settings, in many instances, teachers focus on "controlling rather than teaching them" (Lingard, Martino, Mills, & Bahr, 2002), but it is known that positive student-teacher relationships improve educational outcomes (Derksen, 1995; Brekelmans, Wubbels,& van Tartwijk, 2006). Teachers must be invested in challenging traditional teacher-student paradigms that emphasize power and control and work towards cooperation and partnership with students and with families (Meehan, Hughes, Cavell, 2003). This approach can transform the educational experience for students and teachers. All teachers will encounter challenging students. As you interact with your most challenging students it is important to keep in mind:

- You cannot expect for students to come into your classroom with an open heart and mind if your heart and mind is not open. Be willing to talk to students about how the two of you can best work together to create a positive learning experience and be open to giving previously "problem students" opportunities to prove and redeem themselves.

- Poor student-teacher interactions can foster mistrust in teachers and negative self-image in students. These interactions can have a lasting impact that will follow students throughout their academic career.

- Teachers have to be careful not to base their attitudes toward their students on things they hear from other teachers. While this information might be useful in developing a plan for how to effectively engage and teach students, it should not be used to label or stigmatize them.

REFERENCES

1. Brekelmans, M., Wubbels, T., & Van Tartwijk, J. (2005). Teacher–student relationships across the teaching career. *International Journal of Educational Research, 43*(1), 55-71.

2. Derksen, K. (1995). *Activating instruction: The effects of a teacher-training programme.* Paper presented at the 6th conference of the European Association for Research on Learning and Instruction, Nijmegen, August.

3. Lingard, B., Martino, W., Mills, M., & Bahr, M. (2002). Addressing the educational needs of boys. *Canberra: Australian Government, Department of Education, Science and Training.*

5th Grade

Trust issues

"You cannot teach me if I do not trust you"

Going into 5th grade I had pretty much made up my mind that there were two types of people that I could not trust – the police and teachers. By the age of 10 I had had many negative encounters with both, and in my mind they were one in the same. Neither one was my friend.

After my third grade experience of being held back and placed in Special Education and being treated like a guilty criminal in the fourth grade, I must admit that my new 5th grade teacher had a major task on her hands. She was going to have to reengage me and convince me to care about school again. She was also going to have to go to great lengths to get me to trust her. I don't know if she knew it, but those were her first two priorities if she was going to have success with me and the other kids like me. I had vowed that I would never allow another teacher in my heart again after my past abusive experiences, so I entered her classroom with a closed heart and mind on the first day of school. I just knew that she was going to be like all of the other teachers who had hurt me in the past.

One by one she went around the class and asked us our names and what our interest were. When she got to me, she seemed to take more time, asking me an array of questions. By the end of our conversation she knew a lot about my family and that I wanted to be a professional football player, rapper, singer and actor. Most of my previous teachers never took the time out to really get to know me, nor did they ever take time out for me to get to know them. It was all about the books and sticking to the lesson plans for the day. But this teacher seemed different. She seemed to care about who I was as a person, At least that's what I thought.

Her warmth and patience made me feel more comfortable with her, and little by little I started opening up. Instead of sitting in the back of class day dreaming about sports and music, she had me engaged in what she was teaching, in part because she constantly called on me for answers to her questions and allowed me to ask questions and act things out. I had to be ready at all times because at any moment I knew she would call on me and I didn't want to let her down. I had forgotten what it felt like to answer questions in class and to engage in class discussion, but when I started back it felt so good. It was like a new side of me was being discovered and the old kid who once loved school was being reawakened. Before I knew it I started looking forward to school again and getting my good morning and goodbye hugs from her. Little did I know all of this was about to change.

As I have mentioned before, most of the schools I attended during my school years were located in the suburbs. This is how my mom wanted it, so she did everything she could to find the cheapest rent house or apartment we could afford, to keep me and my brothers in this district. The town we lived in was a small working class suburb of Oklahoma City, and is still as segregated today as it was when I was a kid, but the schools were considered better than the so called failing public schools of Oklahoma City.

My mother just wanted my brothers and I to have the best education we could possibly have. With our best interest at heart, she moved us into a poor neighborhood a few miles from the school I was going to attend. This meant that I was often the only black student in my class and sometimes one of very few black kids in the entire school. I had to endure the many dangers to my psyche inside of the classroom and I was exposed to the many dangers to my psyche outside of the classroom, especially during my walks home.

The dismissal bell rang at 3:25 like every other day of the new school year. I gathered my things and gave my new favorite teacher a goodbye hug and met up with some of my black friends who lived close to me so we could walk home. As we walked across the street from the school parking lot we encountered a policeman who asked us where we were headed. After we told him, he asked us more questions, like were we in any gangs and did we have any drugs or weapons on us? Before I knew it, he had me and my friends against his car, frisking us and searching through our bags. This was happening right across the street from my new school that I had started to love because I felt that the people in it felt the same way about me. But what happened next changed my whole perception of this school and my new favorite teacher.

As the cop searched through our bags some of my

white classmates passed by. Many of them laughed and others asked what I had done, like I was guilty of something. I must admit, I was completely humiliated that I was in this predicament because it did not look good. I was hurt the most when I glanced across the street and saw my classroom teacher who was standing out in front of the school looking at me. She walked outside and another teacher who I didn't know pointed in my direction. When my teacher looked my way I tried to get her attention. I wanted her to come help me get out of this situation but she pretended like she didn't see me, walked to her car, and drove off.

That night, I remember crying in my room and tearing up the homework that she had assigned for the day. I vowed that I would not say another word in her class again. The next morning I showed up to school and I could tell that she knew that I saw her ignoring me. The guilt was all over her face and in the way she interacted with me.

Later that morning she finally spoke to me and

asked for my homework. When I told her that I tore it up she was silent, then she asked me if I wanted to come up to the board and do some math problems. This was something that I usually ran to the board to do, but this time I replied, "I don't feel like it." "Why?" she asked. I replied, "Because yesterday when you saw me being messed with by that cop you just walked away, and wouldn't come over there to help. You wouldn't come and tell him I was not in a gang and that I wasn't a drug dealer, so no, I don't want to!" After my rant she said, "Well Joseph, I'm sorry but that's not my job. I just want to teach and that's what I'm here to do." After that day I completely shut down and did not allow her to teach me anything else and I tried my best to keep her from teaching anyone else.

THINGS I WISH MY TEACHER KNEW

I wish my teacher would have known that is important to understand and be sensitive to the

history and current reality of her students.

Positive student-teacher bonding has been demonstrated to serve as a protective mechanism against academic failure and disciplinary issues (Pianta, Steinberg, & Rollins, 1995). Although my teacher didn't know it, I had a history of being mislabeled and misjudged. This was particularly difficult because many of the people who did this were people that I knew and should have been able to trust. At a very young age I was very aware of how others responded to me, but she was different. She was the one who made me feel loved and at peace every day when I entered her classroom. She was the one that helped to restore my faith in teachers, school and myself. I thought she had my back no matter what. All I wanted her to do when she saw me being profiled was to walk over and check on me. To tell the police officer that I was not a bad kid. I needed her to walk over and let him know that I was a part of a school family that cared about me and that I would never carry a weapon or drugs to school. When she did not take this simple step, I felt betrayed, unloved, and alienated.

Student alienation can lead to academic struggles, issues with social and emotional adjustment, and issues with peer relationships (Coleman, 1961; McCleod, 1995; Stinchcombe, 1969). As teachers, we have to be mindful that our students are complex human beings who have complex lives outside of classrooms. Even when we are not aware of all of their circumstances, we need to take deliberate steps to establish relationships based on mutual respect and trust. This not only helps our students, but it also makes our job easier when we have cooperative and engaged students who love school and learning.

I wish my teacher would have understood that the treatment of her students outside of the classroom was just as important as her treatment of the students in the classroom.

For my peers and myself, we wrestled with outside distractions more than anything else. Many of our neighborhoods and homes were filled with outside noise that kept us from taking the next step to fully reach our highest academic potential. Many of us where surrounded by and immersed in drugs, gangs, violence, generational school failure, poverty and police harassment. What we needed most was a teacher who cared about us inside *and* outside of the classroom.

One of my teacher's biggest mistakes was thinking that if she just instructed me and worked to get my grades and test scores up, she had succeeded. She didn't realize that in order for her to get me to stand up and care about solving those math problems in her classroom, I needed to know and trust that she cared about the life problems I had outside of the classroom.

My teacher did not know that I viewed her in the same way that I viewed the people who lived around me – as an extended family member. Even though we had many issues in our neighborhood, there were still people in the community who looked out for each other. If you needed help you could count on someone to reach out to you. My trust and love for her extended far beyond the classroom, but she just wanted to show up to school and teach and not worry about what happened to me after school when my real life began.

ENGAGEMENT APPROACH

Is it possible to be an educator and an advocate for your students? I believe the answer to that question is, "Yes". The first step to becoming an advocate is broadening the spectrum of what we view as being an educator. An educator is not one who just does what they are told and nothing more – that's a robot. As humans we all have real needs, pains, dreams and desires that must be met and paid attention to. Our students are no different.

We also have real tough decisions to make in life. One of the decisions we have to make as educators is what will we do if and most likely when we see injustices being committed inside and outside of our school to our students? What if these injustices are perpetrated by police officers in our school, out in the community, or other adults in our building? Educators are often trained and encouraged to spot and report abuse by parents and bullying by other students. Very few of us have been trained nor encouraged to speak up about abuse we recognize inside of our schools amongst our ranks. In this regard, many educators are very much like the police, as we are subconsciously and organizationally pressured to 'protect the shield' even when we see one of our peers misusing their power.

Before one can truly become an advocate for their students, you must ask yourself whose side you are on. If you are a 'go with the flow' type of person that will allow questionable practices to exist and never question nor challenge them because they are the organizational cultural norms, then you may not be ready to advocate for anyone except the status quo. But if you are willing to step out there and advocate for your students in the face of resistance; if you are willing to fight for their rights to a quality education as well as their right to a quality life then you are ready.

As educators we have the privilege and responsibility of being the middle men/women between the police and our students. This puts us in a unique position to create bridges for dialogue, healing, reconciliation and understanding. I personally feel like teachers are in the greatest position to bring about social change in the context of bringing everyone in the community together. Traditionally everyone trusts the school teacher, and in many communities that tradition still exists.

Because of the trust that most people in the community have for teachers, we have the power to speak to all parties of a community. We can walk into a police department and speak with them about our students concerns, and we will be heard. We can walk into our classrooms and speak to our students about the concerns the police have, and we will be heard. We can go to our local church and community leaders and be heard, and for that matter we can also speak on the block to the local drug dealers and gang members and they will listen too, because they were once students at the schools where we teach. I personally know this because as a teacher I have done this.

IN SUMMARY

Strong student-teacher relationships are a key component to student success. Having strong supportive relationships with a teacher helps at risk students to feel safer, more competent, and achieve greater academic success. Conversely, conflict with teachers can increase students' risk of disengaging and failing in school (Hamre, 2006).

As we answer the call of our occupational responsibility to prepare our students for life, by often going out of our way to find new material and insight to teach them. We too have a social responsibility to go out of our way to protect them so we can reach them. Part of this protection is holding those accountable who attempt to break their spirits and side track the minds that we are in competition for.

REFERENCES

1. Coleman, J.S. (1961). The Adolescent Society. New York: Press of Glencoe.

2. Crosnoe, R., Johnson, M. K., & Elder, G. H. (2004). Intergenerational bonding in school: The behavioral and contextual correlates of student-teacher relationships. *Sociology of education*, 77(1), 60-81.

3. Hamre, B. K., & Pianta, R. C. (2006). Student-Teacher Relationships.

4. McCleod, J. (1995). Ain't No Making It. Boulder, CO: Westview Press.

5. Pianta, R.C., Steinberg, M.S., Rollins, B. (1995). The first two years of school: Teacher-child relationships and deflections in children's classroom adjustment. *Development and Psychopathology*, 7, 295-312.

6. Stinchecombe, A. (1964). Rebellion in a High School. Chicago: Quadrangle Press.

6th Grade

You Let the Girls Get Away With Everything

"Hurt boys become hurt men. Abused boys become abusive men."

"I really don't think she likes us."

"Me neither."

"Yea, it's always our fault, but man, the girls never get in trouble."

"That's because they are her favorite."

Those were the words often spoken by me and my

friends in elementary school. The start of middle school was a scary, confusing and frustrating time for me and many of my male classmates. We were not quite young men/teenagers, so we were still very immature, but we were no longer little kids either. We were at that awkward 'tweenager' stage. We were at the age when most boys begin searching for their manhood and for who they are in the world. We were going through all of this while trying to balance the very intense, very real feelings that the world was out to get us. At least that's how me and my boys felt about the police and some of our teachers who, unfortunately, happened to be all female. Many of us also had hormones that were raging out of control but we were not that into girls yet, because we were scared of them, but most importantly we were scarred by them, too.

My scarring started during that previous summer, with a girl who was two years older than me and what seemed like two feet taller than me. This girl was my worst nightmare. All of my life, I had heard from my mom, every man I had ever met, and on TV, that a male should never put his hands on a female, no matter what. I believed that, and because of the respect for other people that my mom instilled in me, I abided by that rule. The problem is, no one was telling this girl that no matter what, girls should not put their hands on boys. Unfortunately for me she felt she had free reign to do whatever she wanted to me and I would not, could not do anything back to her, so every day while outside with my friends she always found a reason to pick a fight with me.

We all know what happens when kids think a fight is about to go down. It was like everyone in the neighborhood stopped what they were doing just to see the world star hood fight. I refused to give them the show that they wanted, but this girl was more than happy to do so. That summer I stood by as she punched me in my face, stomach, and kicked me in my groin. It was better to stand there and take it, than to hit her back and feel bad or run away and be embarrassed in front of everyone. The boys in the neighborhood knew that I could fight because many of them had tried me and failed, so they got a kick out watching me get kicked and punched by this girl and not fighting back.

I can't recall how many times I ran home in tears after she beat me up, crying because I felt helpless and frustrated because I could not do anything about it. To avoid the embarrassment of getting beat up by her, I would lie to my mama and brothers that I had been into a fight with a boy. This is where the scarring started, because I began to build up an intense distain for girls, because of the things that I felt they were getting away with. Unfortunately it did not stop there. This was just the beginning.

The one thing I hated about middle school was that the girls were still bigger than most of us and they made sure that we knew it. I guess because I had dealt with being bullied by a girl in elementary school and had more negative than positive experiences with teachers who just so happened to be female, I was more observant about how I was treated by females than the average kid. I found it very confusing how it seemed to always be all boys being sent to the office, missing recess, being suspended, sitting out in the hallway, and having our parents called. I was very aware of these things because I was one of those kids. But the problem was, my male friends and I saw the girls do the same things that we did, and more, but very seldom did they get in trouble in the same way.

I did not understand how the girls, who were bigger than many of the boys, could get away with hitting us, and nothing happened to them. I knew that if one of us had hit them we would have been in a lot of trouble. Yes, in earlier grades I saw the boys hitting girls more frequently, but as we got older in 5th and 6th grade I saw more girls hitting boys and always getting away with this, and many other behaviors. To add to the frustration, whenever one of the boys would try to tell on the girls for hitting, we were told to "toughen up", or "man up". Translation: our feelings were not as important as the girls' feelings, and our classroom was not a safe space where we could freely express ourselves. So we shut down, and that's when the frustrations and anger began to build.

During the class breaks I always noticed the girls gathering around the teacher's desk as they would sit and talk about all things "female". The boys never went up to her desk because truthfully, we didn't feel welcomed. On class breaks we didn't want to sit around. We wanted to get up, walk around and sometimes just be boyish with each other, but she wasn't having it. So we sat there bored. It was never long before we would get into trouble for something, usually something we did out of boredom, anxiousness and out of just being boys.

It was only natural that many of my male peers became extremely disengaged from our female teachers because we felt like they did not like us as much as they liked the girls. We felt that they allowed them to get away with things that we got in trouble for. I will never forget the time that my teacher sent me to the hallway and put her finger in my face and yelled so loud that everyone on the hall could hear her. To this day, that was one of my most humiliating moments at school. In the hood, this would have been considered disrespectful behavior and would have ended in a fight, but because she was my teacher and a female I had to stand there and take my emotional beating silently, "like a man".

We were also disengaged because, it seemed like most of the classroom setup and even the way the teachers taught were more catered towards girls. I remember my 6th grade class looking and smelling like my girl cousins room at her house. There were flowers everywhere and colorful lady bugs on the wall, and the class always smelled like perfume. When I looked around I was not able to see anything that I was interested in or that reminded me of the things that looked like me and my brother's room. It's not that I did not want flowers and lady bugs on the wall, because being a country boy, born on a farm, I loved nature. I just wanted more balance. I wanted to see the things that sparked the imagination and aspirations of most little boys like me. I thought to myself where are the pictures of NBA great Michael Jordan, and star NFL running back from the Dallas Cowboys Emmitt Smith? At least they went to this place called college that they kept mentioning to us. Those lady bugs and flowers on the wall did not.

I was also very frustrated that we would come into school after listening to hip hop and then have to sing songs or say things that I felt were very corny and culturally unresponsive. I understood that those may have been the rules but I wasn't any less upset that I was being forced to sing songs with girls, while I was trying to become a man. There was nothing worse than being age 9, 10, 11 and 12 in search of your manhood and being forced to sit on the floor, criss-cross applesauce and sing songs alongside girls.

All they had to do was really take a look at us and see that we were not completely happy in the over feminized climate. I felt we were not being seen at all, unless we were getting into trouble and then we were under the spotlight.

It wasn't until my teenage years that, I was finally able to come to terms with what I felt was gender inequality towards boys at school and got over my anger towards females altogether. Unfortunately, many of my male friends were not able to shake the anger and grew up to become men who now abuse women.

Note: It is important for me to clarify that in this chapter I am in no way saying that female teachers and girls are responsible for males who abuse females. As I have become an adult and began working with youth I have seen the importance of working with young men to stop violence against women and will continue to work tirelessly to do so. I do, however, feel it is necessary that all genders examine the ways in which we can prevent young men and women from being abusive towards each other. As educators, we have to ask ourselves what role we play in creating emotionally healthy kids who feel equally respected and accepted, and what role do we play in creating emotionally unhealthy kids who feel like they have been hurt and now want to go out and take their pain out on others.

THINGS I WISH MY TEACHER KNEW

Boys are consistently overrepresented when it comes to school discipline. Several studies have found that boys are sent to the office and received disciplinary consequences at higher rates than girls. (Lietz & Gregory, 1978; McFadden et al., 1992; Shaw & Braden, 1990; Skiba et al., 1997; Taylor & Foster,1986). There is evidence that bullying of boys by girls is not uncommon and it is emotionally harmful even into adulthood (Brinson, 2005). Educators have to be cognizant of these facts and work hard to make sure that the policies and practices within their schools are fair and equitable.

I wish my teacher knew that boys and girls learn differently – and this matters.

In the book, *Raising Cain: Protecting the emotional life of boys*, Kindlon and Thompson discuss how behaviors most often identified with girls become the "gold standard" in school classrooms. This leads to boys being treated as "defective girls", rather than as unique individuals with different needs. Increasing evidence proves that while some gender differences are due to socialization, there are real biochemical and biological differences between girls and boys that need to be accounted for in educational settings. For example: male brains are larger, but have fewer connections than female brains, females have more connections in the verbal section of the brain, and the right side of the brain develops more rapidly in males and the left side develops more rapidly in females (James, 2007). What all of this really means is that because there are cognitive, brain based differences between girls and boys, educators have to differentiate their teaching styles to maximize education for all students. This approach will improve the classroom experience for everyone – including the teacher.

I wish she knew that boys are sometimes bullied by girls – and it's not okay.

Teachers can begin to change these trends by understanding that they have a large role to play in how their students – girls and boys – experience and engage in school. Teachers have to be careful not to ignore or minimize aggressive behavior of girls towards boys. In a qualitative study of boys who had been bullied by girls, it was found that the adult men recalling their experiences with bullying by girls had been severely emotionally scarred by these experiences. They also reported being less likely to tell someone about these experiences because of humiliation and fear of being perceived as not being "tough" or "strong" (Brinson, 2005).

Teachers and other adults have to set clear rules and expectations that it is not okay for any person – male or female – to physically or verbally abuse another person. When physical abuse does occur, no matter the gender of the perpetrator, the consequences must be strict and just as important, equal. This creates an environment where everyone can feel safe and respected, and a safe space where boys can feel confident that their feelings are important and valued.

I wish she knew that treating boys and girls differently is harmful

Boys often perceive that they are disciplined more often, shouted at more frequently, and unfairly and unequally punished in comparison to girls (Myhill & Jones, 2006). Classroom observations by researchers have confirmed that teachers often more harshly discipline boys and that poor behaviors by girls often go unnoticed (Pickering, 2007; Jackson & Salisbury, 2001). Teachers need to understand that equitable treatment has to go both ways. Boys need and deserve to feel that they will be treated fairly at school. Otherwise, they will not trust their teachers and administrators and ultimately, their emotional, educational and academic well-being will suffer.

ENGAGMENT APPROACH

The engagement approaches for this chapter are really quite simple. It really boils down to three things: respect, trust, and fairness. In school settings, educators have to be careful to not unfairly punish boys and ignore bad behavior by girls. In addition, teachers should take the time to learn about evidence based differences in the learning styles of boys and work to meet the needs of their male students.

If my teachers had been paying attention, they

would have noticed the direct correlation between the male perception of unfair treatment and the increase in disengagement, aggression, and bad behavior. If they had been listening to our complaints, they would have understood that the hitting and bullying by some of the girls was distressing to us, and they would have done something about it. As you read this, make a commitment that you will treat all of your students fairly and equally, and that you will not tolerate bullying or physical violence against any person. When a male student complains about issues of unfair treatment, listen and legitimately investigate and interrogate your own behaviors and work hard to remedy the situation so that school can be a safe space where your students know that they can come to you and their voices will be heard.

IN SUMMARY

In his book, *Boys adrift: The five factors driving the*

growing epidemic of unmotivated boys and underachieving young men, Leonard Cross identifies the devaluation of masculinity as one of the five factors that contributes to the disengagement of boys in education. In an environment of increasing emphasis on decreasing the harmful effects of hyper-masculinity, or what I would rather call "unhealthy masculinity", there has been no emphasis on defining what healthy masculinity is, so that men can model this behavior for boys. Instead, there has been an unrealistic emphasis on "gender neutrality" which is usually not neutral at all. It sometimes looks more like trying to sell "feminization" as gender neutrality. It sometimes looks like encouraging girls and boys to play with the same toys. It often looks like the complete erasure of the fact that boys and girls are not exactly alike – nor should they be. The focus should be on gender equality – not on gender erasure. This practice is proving harmful for boys in particular. Teachers can begin to improve this situation by following these simple tips:

- Understand that boys and girls have different learning styles and behavior patterns. Make room for these differences so that boys feel safe engaging and participating in the classroom.

- Do not discourage or pathologize healthy masculinity. Boys and girls are different – and that's okay. Having a balance between masculine, feminine, and yes, even truly gender neutral classroom practices is healthy for everyone.

- Do not tolerate aggression by girls towards boys. It is not funny, cute, or a joke. Boys who report girl bullies should not be encouraged to "be tough" or "man up". As a victim of bullying I personally know how hurtful it can be and the very real, long-term consequences it brings. And if we are to be fair in our practices and agents of change when it comes to stopping violence against women. We must educate all kids that bullying is not ok and not excuse or ignore anyone because of their gender.

REFERENCES

1. Brinson, S.A. (2005). Boys don't tell on sugar-and-spice-but-not-so-nice girl bullies. reclaiming children and youth, 14(3), 169-174.

2. Jackson, D. & Salisbury, J. (1996) Why should secondary schools take working with boys seriously?, *Gender & Education*, 8(1), 103–11

3. James, A. N. (Ed.). (2007). Teaching the male brain: How boys think, feel, and learn in school. Corwin Press.

4. Kindlon, D., & Thompson, M. (2009). *Raising Cain: Protecting the emotional life of boys.* Ballantine Books.

5. Lietz, J. J., & Gregory, M. K. (1978). Pupil race andsex determinants of office and exceptional education referrals. *Educational Research*

Quarterly, 3(2), 61-66.

6. McFadden, A. C., Marsh, G. E., Price, B. J., & Hwang, Y. (1992). A study of race and gender bias in the punishment of handicapped school children. *Urban Review*, 24, 239-251.

7. Myhill, D., & Jones, S. (2006). 'She doesn't shout at no girls': pupils' perceptions of gender equity in the classroom. *Cambridge Journal of Education*, 36(1), 99-113.

8. Pickering, J. (1997) *Raising boys' achievement* (Stafford, Network Educational Press).

9. Sax, L. (2009). *Boys adrift: The five factors driving the growing epidemic of unmotivated boys and underachieving young men.* New York: Basic Books.

10. Shaw, S. R., & Braden, J. P. (1990). Race and gender bias in the administration of corporal punishment. *School Psychology Review*, 19, 378-383.

11. Skiba, R. J., Michael, R. S., Nardo, A. C., &

Peterson, R. L. (2002). The color of discipline: Sources of racial and gender disproportionality in school punishment. *The urban review*, 34(4), 317-342.

12. Skiba, R. J., Peterson, R. L., & Williams, T. (1997). Office referrals and suspension: Disciplinary intervention in middle schools. *Education and Treatment of Children*, 20(3), 295-315.

13. Sommers, C. H. (2001). *The war against boys: How misguided feminism is harming our young men.* Simon and Schuster.

14. Taylor, M.C., & Foster, G. A. (1986). Bad boys and school suspensions: Public policy implications for black males. *Sociological Inquiry*, 56, 498-506.

15. Tyre, P. (2009). *The trouble with boys: A surprising report card on our sons, their problems at school, and what parents and educators must do.* Three Rivers Press.

7th Grade

Do You Know the Odds?

"Shooting down my dreams is the same as shooting me because I am my dreams."

It was the first day of school. I was now in 7th grade, and for the first time in my life I had a male teacher who seemed to be really cool. I wondered who his favorite football and basketball team was. That's the first thing I wondered about him, as I watched his every move. The second thing I wondered was, "Is he like the other adult males that I had come across in my life?" I really hoped so, because I had had some great experiences with male role models up to this point.

From the time I was old enough to walk and then run, sports had played a major part of my life. Although I was really into music and theater, sports had played and even larger role than the arts, because of the area of the country I grew in.

Where I come from, sports were king, and if you were a great athlete you were a king too. The stories I heard about my dad and mom, and how they were both great athletes in their respective towns were legendary. Everywhere I went in East Texas people spoke to me about my dad. They told me that he was a great high school football player. He was so good that he later got invited to play for the Dallas Cowboys, but he could not overcome his addictions. When I spoke to people in my mom's home town I heard the same things about her. People told me that she was a star basketball player as well as track runner who held records for years in the town she grew up in in Oklahoma.

Great athletic genes were passed down to me and

my brothers from both sides of our family so it was only natural that we gravitated to sports and excelled in whatever we played. When I started playing sports, my life truly started changed. During my sixth grade year I won the All-City wrestling championship as well as the All-City championship in The 100 and 200 hundred meter sprints in Track, but it was my football skills as a running back that brought attention and popularity my way.

It's amazing how quickly things can turn around when people find out you are a great athlete. I went from being a kid no one wanted to be bothered with to the most well-known and sought after, overnight. I had finally found something that made me feel good about myself and gave me a since of pride. Although I was just as good at singing, rapping, and playing instruments, I was growing up in Oklahoma City, not New York City, so sports, mainly football, was my ticket. It was through sports that I was provided shelter and comfort from being considered an outsider who was doomed to fail. Instead, I was considered the most popular kid with a future. I had not been successful in anything else in school, so from my 6th grade year on, I decide I was going to go after the only thing that I knew and had had any success in.

My seventh grade teacher found out that I was a great athlete after he and many of the other teachers came to our schools first home football game. During the game I scored 5 touch downs and we won the game in a blowout. Over the next few weeks my popularity began to grow as I helped my team win more and more games and scored multiple touchdowns. The town was abuzz, and if you are winning the buzz becomes a feverish pitch. Yes, it was only Jr. High School football, but to the people around town it was everything.

We had just won the biggest game of the season and were preparing for our crosstown rivals. When I walked into the classroom and my teacher started asking all the students what they wanted to become when we grew up. One-by-one my classmates rambled off their aspirations. When my turn came, I said I wanted to become a professional football player. He replied, "Hey Joseph, that's not a real goal. Do you know the odds of making it to the NFL? You should pursue something more practical. It's probably not gone to happen for you bud." After the kids stopped laughing, I asked him how he knew I was not going to make it. He said, "Because you're barely passing your classes, so you may never even make it to college to play football."

My teacher had nothing negative to say about the kid who said he wanted to be President, when the odds of becoming President are way more unlikely. There is only one President every 4 or 8 years. And there had only been 42 President's in the history of the country up to this point! But there are 2,000 football players who get to play in the NFL every year. He didn't have anything negative to say to the kids who said they wanted to become astronauts or millionaires either, as if these were more likely goals. He did not knock the dreams of the kids who wanted to become CEO's of Fortune 500 companies, ignoring the fact that those jobs are few in number as well. I knew he had singled me out because I wanted to be a professional athlete.

After his assault on my football dream, I never again felt safe telling him my dreams or talking to him about the things that I loved. I also no longer desired to listen to him talk about how important it was for us to get an education, especially if getting one meant that I had to give up what I loved.

THINGS I WISH MY TEACHER KNEW

That dream that all students are told to go after. That dream that all teachers are told to encourage their students to pursue. That dream of going to college. Most athletes have one thing in common: they have achieved that dream. One hundred percent of NFL Players have attended college because you cannot go to the NFL without playing in college. Recently, the same is true of NBA basketball players. While a lot of attention has been paid to academic underperformance among athletes, statistics show that student athletes obtain college degrees at record rates. In fact, according to the NCAA:

> *"84 percent of Division I student-athletes who entered college in 2007 graduated – the highest rate ever. Division I student-athletes continue to outperform their peers in the general student body, when compared using the federal graduation rate."*

This fact should not be ignored. For many students, college athletics is a very real and viable way to get into and finance a college education. While this may not be their main motivation for wanting to play sports, I am a living witness that this can change. I literally only attended college because I wanted to play sports. I now have a Bachelor's degree, a Master's degree, and I am working on my PhD at an Ivy League

University, so I made it to "The League" after all. Sports were my path to education, and I am not ashamed to let others know, and I am not alone. Rather than having a negative reaction to students who love sports and want to play them professionally, encourage them to use sports as an opportunity to create a better life for themselves – whether they "make it" in professional sports or not. The realest odds are, that even if they do not make it in sports they will make it in something other than sports because of the work ethic and discipline they developed while playing.

I wish my teacher knew that one of the biggest reasons that my friends and I looked up to athletes is because they followed their dreams.

When I was a first year Special Education and Life Skills teacher in Dallas, TX, I still had a dream of playing football professionally. While I was teaching that year, I was also training very hard to make an NFL team. At the beginning of the school year, I put in my leave request for the days of the NFL football combine in Atlanta, GA. I never missed work, came on time every day, and made it a point to save my vacation days so that when the time came for me to pursue my dream there would be no obstacles. At the end of the school year, when the time came to go to the football tryouts, my Principal somehow caught wind that the reason I was taking vacation days was so that I could try out for the NFL. He retroactively denied my leave request, and warned me that if I attended the tryouts, my contract would not be renewed the next year.

As you can imagine, I was faced with a terrible dilemma. I loved my job and I loved my students. I also loved football. I appealed this decision with the Teachers Union, but I knew the appeal would not come in time for me to attend the tryout. When my students heard what I was going through, there was an amazing outpouring of support. See, I was known as the cool teacher, but I was also the inspirational teacher who encouraged all of the students to go after their dreams. Every day during the week before the tryout, I had at least half a dozen students approach me and say things like:

- "Mr. Mathews, all year, you've been telling us to pursue our dreams. If you don't go, everything you said to us was a lie!"

- "We love you and we want you here, but I'd rather see you playing in the NFL because I know you'll be happy and that will give me hope."

- "You're our hero!"

After hearing all of these things from my students, how could I not go after my dream? When I returned to school after the tryout, you would not believe the reaction of the students. It was like I was a celebrity. Even though my students knew that I would not be returning the next year as a result of my decision, they were so happy and so proud of me. They would rather see their favorite teacher stand up for what he believed in and pursue his dream than to stay and give up on his goals.

I tell this story to give teachers a better perspective on what it really means when students look up to athletes. It is not just because they are famous and make a lot of money. Athletes represent something that many kids, especially kids in the inner city long for – an opportunity to make dreams come true. Athletes are inspirational because they go after something that seems unobtainable – and they get it. This is what most students see and aspire to. Rather than discouraging this, find ways to incorporated this into your discussions with your students who love sports. They will likely open up to you in ways that you never imagined. I know I would have.

I wish my teacher knew that playing sports has a positive impact on students – whether they go on to play professionally.

Students who participate in sports have been found

to experience less depression; use drugs less often, have higher GPAs, and have better relationships with their parents than students who do not (Melnick et al., 1992; Field et al., 2001; Scheuer et al., 2003). Whether students go on to play professional sports, playing team sports can be a powerful motivator for students to maintain good grades and good behavior. Some research has also found that sports participation helps to keep at-risk students engaged in school (Melnick et al., 1992). For my peers and I, sports also taught us self-discipline and the value of teamwork. Personally, sports were often the only reason I did not drop out of school, and when I did drop out, they were the main reason I returned.

Whether educators like the facts I have outlined, the reality is that we can use sports as a way to reach student athletes. It is actually counter-productive to outline all of the reasons that sports may not be a realistic career path. Trust me, you will not be the first person to tell the star football player in your class about the odds against making it in professional sports. Why not try a different approach? Why not use it as a point of connection and a way to keep some of your most disengaged students engaged in class? You might be surprised at the positive results.

ENGAGEMENT APPROACH

Teachers should have the goal of getting to know their students and learning about their hopes dreams and aspirations. This can be a powerful way of connecting with students and finding ways to make school more interesting. When students are less than motivated in your class, they can be reminded of these goals and how what they are learning in school connects with who and what they want to be in the future. Creative, individualized instruction can be used to incorporate aspects of the students' goals in the lessons. Students can be given class projects and assignments that tie into their future goals.

What if my teacher had introduced me to the hundreds upon hundreds of sports careers that I could have pursued if my aspiration of playing professional sports did not work out? What if he had made the connection between school and sports by showing me how I could have a professional career in sports even if I did not make it to the NFL? How powerful would it have been if we understood that the athletes we looked up to, actually went to college and were once 7th graders like us? What if he exposed me to the fact that the people I watched talk about sports on TV all day actually went to college in order to do so?

IN SUMMARY

Teachers have a huge influence on how their students feel about their future and their dreams. As educators, we can ground students without killing their dreams. As a Life Skills teacher at a school in Washington, DC, I took a group of students who wanted to be singers and rappers on a field trip to the Black Entertainment Television (BET) offices in DC and to a taping of a popular television show on the network in New York City. Rather than pointing out what the entertainers did, we discussed all of the other jobs that we saw during our trip. Students saw videographers, lighting and sound technicians, directors, and producers. At the BET headquarters, they had the opportunity to speak with Program Directors, attorneys, public relations professionals and business managers. They left truly inspired that they could have a career in the music business. Many of the aspiring rappers walked away feeling as if they knew more about the music industry and some even walked away wanting to be behind the camera. I know this experience opened their eyes and had a profound impact on their lives. In fact, one of my students is currently in Film School in Houston, TX! As you interact with your students, handle their dreams with care. And remember:

✐ While it is important for us to teach and encourage our students to be goal oriented, it is not important that students know exactly "what they want to be when they grow up". We can help students to identify their talents and skills and show them ways to use these talents to become who they want to be in the future.

✐ Don't kill your student's dreams. Whatever they say they want to do in the future, find positive ways to encourage and if necessary provide alternatives to these dreams without making them feel like their dreams are not obtainable. They have plenty of people trying to discourage them. Don't be one of those people.

REFERENCES

1. Brutlag Hosick, M. (2014, October 3). Student-athletes earn diplomas at record rate. Retrieved from http://www.ncaa.org/about/resources/media-

center/news/student-athletes-earn-diplomas-record-rate

2. Field, T., Diego, M., & Sanders, C. E. (2001). Exercise is positively related to adolescents' relationships and academics. Adolescence.

3. Melnick, M. J., Sabo, D. F., & Vanfossen, B. (1992). Educational effects of interscholastic athletic participation on African-American and Hispanic youth. *Adolescence*, (27), 295-308.

4. Scheuer, L. J., & Mitchell, D. (2003). Does physical activity influence academic performance. *The New PE and Sport Dimension*, 12.

8th Grade

The Grinch Who Wouldn't Smile Until Christmas

"Nothing great comes from a package delivered with a frown."

"What is wrong with this man? Why won't he smile?" This is what I thought to myself because the teacher always seemed upset or scared of us. He wouldn't talk to us about anything other than school work, and never once did we see him smile.

Like most eight graders around the country, we were admittedly really talkative. We were full of hormones as well as a little hard headed when it came to listening. It wasn't that we wanted to be disrespectful for the sake of being disrespectful. We just had a lot going on and needed someone to understand us, but we also needed more understanding about things going on around us and to us.

From the first day of school and every day after, I walked in my new English teacher's classroom and just thought to myself, "Man, there is something about this dude that I can't quite put my finger on". He was a little… different. Not in a cool teacher kind of way, but in a new teacher who is scared as hell kind of way. It seemed like there was always something that he wanted to say to us, but it would never come out. Never in my years of going to school had I seen a teacher be so distant from the students, while at the same time asking them to be open with him. He wanted for us to be an open book to him and within a few days of school starting asked us to write about ourselves. The problem is, we did not know *him*.

When I asked him to tell us something about

himself, all of my classmates collectively agreed, but all he told us was his name, and the college he went to. Then he told me to get back to work. After a few minutes I raised my hand again and asked him, "Why do you want us to write about ourselves? What are you gonna do with this information?" He didn't know that by this time in my life I had already been to juvenile detention a few times, so I was very suspicious of teachers and police. He proceeded to tell me that this was just so he could get to know us, so I once again asked him, "Who are you? Because man, you have not smiled since school started, and if I can just be honest with you sir, I don't feel comfortable writing things about myself because you remind me of a detention officer or an undercover police officer." After that I gathered my things and walked to our schools detention office, where he sent me for the rest of the class period. He sent my assignment for the day and I was supposed to finish my writing assignment about myself.

At the end of the period, the school detention officer asked me to see what I had written. When he saw that I had done nothing he told me that I would have to stay until I wrote something. I thought it was really unfair that I was being forced to be an open book and my teacher was not. Why should I be forced to make myself completely vulnerable while he remained anonymous? To get out of detention, I figured I would make up a story so everyone would get what they wanted. They could think they won by getting me to read about me, and I could get them to leave me alone.

When I returned to class the next day, my teacher really thought that he had won. In my mind, I felt like he had lost because he still didn't know me, but in all truthfulness I felt like I had lost too, because I still did not know who he was. For the rest of that year we remained in a stalemate. Every day I walked into his class, he had a stone face like a prison guard and I completely blocked out everything he said. Truth is, I could not even stand to look at him. I hated that he never smiled and would not let down his prison guard act, which made me feel like he thought we were prisoners. More importantly, I was longing for him to share his story with us like so many of the adults in my past had done. I needed that to feel more comfortable with opening up to him. I was really asking him to make himself vulnerable so it would be okay for me to be vulnerable. I just wanted to be inspired by him.

As it turns out, he really did not want to be there in the first place. He was just using us to get some teaching experience so he could go to graduate school, which is what he ended up doing. He is now probably a professor somewhere teaching other teachers how to teach and passing himself off as an expert.

THINGS I WISH MY TEACHER KNEW

I wish my teacher knew that I had opened myself up to teachers in the past, and it didn't end well.

In the past, when I had opened up to teachers, I ended up either getting burned, having what I told them used against me, or worse having them downplay the pain I expressed. If my teacher expected me to open up, he was going to have to give a little. In a study that examined how African American students defined culturally relevant teaching, they identified three characteristics: 1) creation of loving bonds, 2) community and family type learning environments, and 3) fun and creative learning environments (Howard, 2001). Also, students who feel that they have an intimate relationship with their teachers characterized by trust, out of class communication, and emotional closeness perform better academically (Dobransky et al., 2004). What this suggests is that what students really want and need is to have a *relationship* with their teachers. This only makes sense. In any other relationship, we need communication and trust in order to be successful in that relationship. Teachers' relationships with their students are no different.

ENGAGEMENT APPROACH

Teachers have the right to a personal life outside of school and their students. I am in no way suggesting otherwise. I am however suggesting that as educators we have to open up and share a little bit of our world with our students, because at the end of the day, we are building relationship. These relationships have intrinsic value. But they also have major implications for our students' academic success. It's really very simple. Let your students get to know you. When you have your student's complete interest surveys or write "about me" reports, you should complete and share one as well. This small gesture will go a long way in letting your students know that you are in this together. You are letting them know that you care and that you want to be a part of their life.

SUMMARY

The gist of what we have been talking about up to this point really boils down to one thing – relationships. Students need to feel secure and have good relationships with the people in their inner circle. You, as their teacher, are in their inner circle. On many days, your students will spend more of their day with you than they will with their own parents. Give your students a sense of safety and belonging by showing them that you want to be in their lives. Remember:

- Let your students get to know you so that they have an understanding and appreciation of who you are,
- When you ask students to share details about their lives, be open, nonjudgmental, and loving. Then...share something about your own life.
- Having open, honest, trusting relationships with your students helps to improve their academic performance. What better reason to be more

intentional about having great relationships with our them?

REFERENCES

1. Dobransky, N. D., & Frymier, A. B. (2004). Developing teacher-student relationships through out of class communication. Communication Quarterly, 52(3), 211-223.
2. Howard, T. C. (2001). Telling their side of the story: African-American students' perceptions of culturally relevant teaching. The Urban Review, 33(2), 131-149.

9th Grade

Bracing for You to Leave

"Teachers are like Oklahoma weather; if you don't like them just wait awhile and they will change."

My peers and I had experienced teachers coming in and out of our lives throughout our school experience. In our minds, we had very little motivation to do what our teachers told us to do when we knew they were eventually going to leave us. Most would argue that we should have done what we were supposed to do because it was just the right thing to do. I couldn't agree more, but in our minds, we were doing the right thing. We were protecting ourselves.

Mr. B. was a first year teacher, and from the first day of school I knew he was going to be mad cool. It was not just because he was the youngest teacher at the school, because in the years leading up to this point, my older teachers had been the most effective at reaching and teaching me.

I had never had a math teacher who knew how to connect solving a math problem to solving a life problem. It was the most amazing thing ever. I don't know if he had done his research on me, but he knew exactly how to engage and guide me into doing my math work and performing at my highest level.

Part of his approach was that he always used real world examples that I could relate to and he always spoke about the different careers and fields where we could use our math skills. This approach made math more relevant and inspired me to work harder. The thing that made him the most special was that he was not afraid to speak up for his students, and this made him a hero to us. I had never had a teacher who would say something when they saw me or another student being mistreated, mischaracterized or misunderstood by another teacher. Mr. B. did just that, and he won me over. It felt like he was one of us and I allowed my wall to come down so he could teach me.

I was a freshman, so it was good to know that I was going to have someone who got me – and I got him. Our relationship was one that most would have never imagined, because he was a cowboy hat and boot wearing white man, who also wore tight Wrangler jeans long before skinny jeans were in fashion. Esthetically and culturally we were as different as could be. But relationally we were as close as any teacher I had ever had because I knew he cared. And then it happened.

Like every other morning I walked into his class and sat down ready to learn when he walked in and said he needed to talk to us. Mr. B. was never at a loss for words, nor did he ever stutter, so when he started struggling to get his words out I knew something was really wrong. At first I was braced to hear him say that one of our classmates had died. But then he said, "Today will be my last day. I have taken a job out of state." You could have heard a pin drop. Thankfully the news he had was not about the death of a classmate, but it felt like a death, especially to me, because I had not let many people in, and now the one teacher that I had let in was leaving at the end of the day.

I can't express how much we were in shock. For the rest of the day we just sat there watching the clock, knowing that when we returned to his class for our last period of the day, we would most likely never see him again. Upon returning to our homeroom for 6th period, we started asking him questions. Many kids were noticeably upset at him and searching for answers. It turns out, he was leaving to go to graduate school, just like the teacher I had from the previous year. The more we asked him questions the more we understood that he was there because he needed more experience before he went back to school. The new job he landed was in the same city where he was planning on going to school. It wasn't that we felt like he should not try to better himself. My classmates and I were just sad that his leaving caught us off guard. We just wanted him to be up front and open with us, so we could have a choice to let him in knowing he would soon be gone.

THINGS I WISH MY TEACHER KNEW

I wish my teacher knew that not being honest about his intention to leave sooner made us feel used and abandoned.

Teachers have every right to pursue their dreams and further their education. I have had to leave positions in the past for this very reason. What teachers have to understand is that kids often get attached to their teachers and come to rely on them as caregivers and nurturers.

There was no worse feeling than opening up to a teacher, like one would open up in a new relationship, only to find out that the person you gave your heart to had planned on leaving all along. For many adults being left by someone we love and trust really hurts and takes a long time to get over. Imagine what many of the kids in struggling urban areas go through as they experience many losses in their home life as well as school life on a consistent basis.

When I had a teacher I really liked, it was often still very hard for me to let my guard down. I would often wonder if they were here to stay for a while or if they were here to play games with my heart and leave? Very few of my teachers passed the test. Mr. B. did, so when he left so suddenly I felt extremely betrayed and more hardened towards whoever would be my next teacher.

Educational relationships are very much like any other good relationship in that they are grounded in trust and communication. If there is no trust there can be no growth. I know that leaving was very hard for Mr. B. to do because I know he truly cared about us. It does not change the fact the he and the school did not communicate with us that he would be leaving until the day he left. They didn't give us time to process and allow us a fair chance to protect our hearts. Unlike many of my other classmates, I had been through this all of my life so I was used to it and I kind of suspected it. But I felt like he owed us more. He had asked us to be open with him and we did. He asked us to give him a chance to teach us and we gave him that chance. I personally had every reason to not trust him, based on my past experiences of teachers leaving me high and dry, but I and many others allowed him into our hearts. It was so disappointing that they could in good conscience not tell us about his plans to leave.

Because of the way that education is changing, so many people are transitioning in and out of the field. As one who works with youth and cares about their wellbeing, I think we owe it to students and their families to be up front about our short- and long-term intentions. Some teachers have told me that it will only set a teacher up for failure if students know that they will be leaving, but I believe that it will work in the teachers favor if they are real with their students from the beginning and supported through the process by the school administration. I know to some this may sound counter intuitive, but the greatest benefit from a teacher telling students that they will be leaving is the emotional health and wellbeing of the students, the ones who will be left behind.

Not giving students the benefit of knowing when their teacher will leave in advance can make them even more untrusting and guarded towards future teachers long after the old teacher has gone, which will have an adverse effect on student outcomes and the overall school culture. No matter how difficult it may be or how scary it sounds I believe having an open dialogue with our students will actually work in the favor of the over health of a school. By doing this many schools and teachers can build a real sense of community. A community that is based on openness and transparency with our students and their families.

ENGAGEMENT APPROACH

Looking back on my years as a disengaged student, I wish many of the schools that I attended with high teacher turnover rates would have created a space where teachers who were new could come and share with the students why they wanted to come teach at our school. I also wish that there was a space where teachers who were leaving could come and share with students and allow them to engage in a Q&A session. I feel like this would have helped us to process and cope better with the life changes that we would have to grow up and face ourselves one day.

Teachers who come to teach at urban schools, or who will be teaching urban students need to be better prepared and informed about the challenges and differences that they are going to encounter so they are less likely to leave in the middle of a school year. Kids who already have trust and abandonment issues need time to process and come to terms with teachers leaving. This should not be taken lightly as it can have long-term consequences on the students we are entrusted to nurture.

IN SUMMARY

Besides the emotional toll that teachers leaving can have on students, we know that high teacher turnover has an effect on student achievement (Boyd et al., 2005; Kane et al., 2006; Rivkin et al. 2005; Rockoff, 2004; Ronfeldt et al., 2013). Teachers who have to leave to take new jobs, further their education, or deal with life transitions should keep in mind that their student's feelings need to be considered and handled with care. Teachers who plan on teaching at a school short term should ask themselves:

- Do you engage in any community and trust building exercises with students?
- Do you create space for discussion to share your plans for the future with your students?
- What do you feel are some of the pros of sharing your plans to leave?
- If you were in a similar situation as a student how would you have wanted your school to handle a teacher leaving?

REFERENCES

1. Boyd, D., Grossman, P., Lankford, H., Loeb, S., & Wyckoff, J. (2008). *Who leaves? Teacher attrition and student achievement* (No. w14022). National Bureau of Economic Research.

2. Boyd, D., H. Lankford, S. Loeb and J. Wyckoff (2005) "Explaining the Short Careers of High Achieving Teachers in Schools with Low-

Performing Students," *American Economic Review Proceedings* 95(2), 166-171.

3. Kane, T., J. Rockoff and D. Staiger (2006) "What Does Certification Tell Us about Teacher Effectiveness? Evidence from New York City" NBER W Rivkin, S., E. Hanushek, and J. Kain (2005) "Teachers, Schools, and Academic Achievement" *Econometrica*, 73(2), 417-458.

4. Rockoff, Jonah (2004). "The Impact of Individual Teachers on Student Achievement: Evidence from Panel Data," *American Economic Review Proceedings* 94 (2): 247-252.orking Paper 12155, April 2006.

5. Ronfeldt, M., Loeb, S., & Wyckoff, J. (2013). How teacher turnover harms student achievement. American *Educational Research Journal*, 50(1), 4-36.

10th Grade

Why are you afraid to let me speak?

"A silent education is a violent education."

The older I got, it seemed like the more trouble came my way. The Crips and Bloods were now ingrained into our day to day life in the neighborhood and the police were now more aggressive towards us as me and my friends started looking like young men. Because I lived on the poor black side of town but attended the rich, white high schools on the other side I had a multi-layered perspective that many others did not have.

Most of my friends who lived around me went to school on the black side of town. But because I had turned into a well-known, talented athlete, some concessions were made for me and I was able to attend school across town. That did not prevent me from being exposed to challenges that existed in my neighborhood, but rather expanded the challenges that I had to deal with. Instead of just dealing with the gangs in my neighborhood, I had to travel across town and deal with racism and cops constantly pulling me over and treating me as if I did not belong. I experienced the aggressive actions by the police who patrolled the community that I lived in and when I went to school across town I experienced those same aggressive actions.

This mistreatment caused me to feel anger toward the police and the racist culture in my community. This all came to a head on one fateful April night when I returned home from track practice and turned on the nightly news and saw the L.A. riots taking place. All night I watched as kids the same age as I was vented their anger and frustration about the way they had been treated by police and systemic racism. I had never witnessed anything like this in my lifetime. As a teenager I had experienced the same treatment that those youth in L.A. had experienced. In many ways my experiences were much worse because I was also growing up in an ultraconservative state that had very little social programs for poor kids. And unlike the black people in L.A., black people in Oklahoma were so outnumbered that they were afraid to speak out about how we felt we were being mistreated.

The next morning after the riots started, I remember talking to some of my friends in the neighborhood before I headed across town for school. It was not surprising that they were upset that the police had gotten away with yet another brutality case caught on video. Many of my neighborhood friends had dropped out if school and were ready to go to war but had no one to lead them. Many more just wanted to express themselves but had no one to listen to them.

After spending a few moments with my homies who were outside hanging on the block talking about what was going on in the country, I headed across town to school where every one of my teachers and white classmates acted like nothing was happening. The police, on the other hand, were very much attentive to what was going on. They had become more aggressive toward me and the other black males in my community as if we were the ones that had gotten away with getting caught on camera beating someone. I can't count how many times we were pulled over and pulled out of our car that week, but I remember it happening a lot. To this day I am so thankful, yet surprised, that I survived the amped up aggression towards us.

What I remember more than anything was the culture of silence that I was expected to operate under at school. The week of the Rodney King riots was one of the loneliest weeks I have ever had as a teen in school. Here I was, hurting and having so much to say about what was going on around me and to me, but I was being forced to go on with business as usual. This was the beginning of what would be a 3 year storm through high school. I started realizing that my teachers were either not willing, were unable, or did not care to engage the many challenges that were happening to me outside of class that were very much effecting my in class performance.

THINGS I WISH MY TEACH KNEW

I wish my teacher knew that it was hard for me to care about education when it had nothing to do with what was currently happening to me.

If we are unwilling to address issues that are critically important to our students they will disengage from our classrooms because they won't see the connection between what they are experiencing and what we are teaching. How important do you expect students think that learning about the Constitution is, when they feel like their Constitutional rights are being violated, but no one will affirm those feelings? How important is math, when the economic realities of many of our students mean that they often don't have food to eat or a stable place to live? We have to teach in a way that connects students with the material and shows them how they can change and impact their own lives. And not by just stating that if they get their education they can "get out" of their neighborhood or their current circumstances (more on this later), but rather, in a way that demonstrates that they can change and improve their current circumstances with the knowledge they are gaining.

We also have to be willing to address the issues that are important to our students, just because they are important to them and we care about their feelings and experiences. When a kid knows that you care about them they will open up to you and it will make your job so much easier. If their concerns are being discussed and addressed, their minds will be clearer and they will be better able to focus when it comes time to learn the lessons we have outlined in our curriculum.

ENGAGEMENT APPROACH

Schools have not just the right, but also the obligation, to create an atmosphere of intellectual and political freedom that uses genuine public controversies to help students discuss and envision political possibilities. Addressing public controversies in schools not only is more educative than quashing or ignoring differences it also enhances the quality of decision-making by ensuring that multiple and competing views about controversial political issues are aired, fairly considered, and critically evaluated (Hess, 2009, p. 6).

Your students are more aware of what's going on

in the world then you might think. When something happens that fundamentally changes our country or the world, ignoring these issues does not mean that they do not have an impact on our kids. For example, in light of recent spate of killings of unarmed black people including Trayvon Martin, Michael Brown, Renisha McBride, Eric Garner, Natasha McKenna, Freddie Gray, and seven year old Aiyana Stanley-Jones, it is difficult to imagine not addressing these issues in the classroom. Our students are watching. They are sad. They are scared. And they are waiting for us to acknowledge this and give them an opportunity to speak.

My teachers never thought about how I, a black male in a predominantly white environment, might be feeling about police officers getting away with beating a black man on video. I was hurt and disgusted by this. Your students will be too, if you fail to acknowledge how they identify with 17 year old Trayvon Martin and 19 year old Renisha McBride. These young people were the same age as many high school Juniors and Seniors and given that many of our students have had unpleasant encounters with police and would-be vigilantes, they need to know that we care about how they feel and what they have to say about these issues. Their voices need and deserve to be heard.

SUMMARY

Incorporating current events, particularly those events that might be considered controversial, is a key component to helping students grapple with their own reality, empathize with others, think critically and actively participate in a democratic society (Hess, 2002; Hess and Posselt, 2002; Rossi, 1995, Waterson, 2009). Don't ignore issues that impact your students. Don't discourage critical dialogue and problem solving. The educational experience of your students and your own educational experience as a teacher will be so much better for it. Remember:

- Kids watch the news and engage in social media. They know what's going on and they have an opinion about it. Use your classroom as an opportunity for them to express their feelings and hone their critical thinking and problem solving skills.

- Ignoring issues that directly impact your students makes them feel like you do not care about what is happening to them and around them. Show them that you care creating a safe space for them to talk about their experiences and feelings.

REFERENCES

1. Hess, D. (2002). Discussing controversial public policy issues in secondary social studies classrooms: Learning from skilled teachers. *Theory and Research in Social Education*, 30(1), 10-41.

2. Hess, D. E. (2009). Controversy in the classroom: The democratic power of discussion. Routledge.

3. Hess, D., & Posselt, J. (2002). How high school students experience and learn from the discussion of controversial public issues. *Journal of Curriculum and Supervision*, 17(4), 283-314.

4. Rossi, J. A. (1995). In-depth study in an issues-oriented social studies classroom. *Theory and Research in Social Education*, 23(2), 88-120.

5. Waterson, R. A. (2009). The examination of pedagogical approaches to teaching controversial public issues: Explicitly teaching the Holocaust and comparative genocide. *Social Studies Research and Practice*, 4(2), 1-24.

11th Grade

Why Should I Stay in an Abusive Relationship?

"You want me to care about what happened in the past and what will happen in the future but will not care about what is happening to me now."

The summer after my sophomore year was one of the hottest three months I can remember in Oklahoma City. Given the current racial tensions that existed in the country, everyone was on edge; the police, the Crips and Bloods, and the people who were just bystanders. By July, it became apparent that there was a good reason for all of us to be on guard because our city saw record numbers of violent crimes and murders committed by gang members and police alike.

The city was on fire and we were in the middle of what seemed like a war. That summer in particular, I lost more friends to drive-by shootings than I had the previous two summers. I truly believe it had a lot to do with the spilled over frustration from the acquittal of the cops from the Rodney King beating as well as the drug wars that were taking place in Oklahoma City and many other cities.

It did not help that on every music stationed we turned to all we heard was "gansta rap" and every movie that came out was about gang life; *Boys in the Hood, Menace to Society,* and *Colors.* But unlike the other cities that were experiencing the same onslaught of negative music and movie images, Oklahoma did not have very many social programs being provided to us that could be used as a preventative buffer from the streets. We either had sports or the streets. I, and many of my friends who did play sports, didn't have a choice because our families were banging and we were automatically considered to be in a gang too.

After spending my summer witnessing drive-by shootings and being harassed by the police, school started, but unfortunately the killing did not stop. The first two months of my junior year were excruciating as it became increasingly more difficult to stay focused on school when so many of my friends were dying around me. It was during this time in my life that I just knew my life was going to end. I didn't know how or when, I just felt it was going to end just like it had ended for so many of my friends. I would ask myself, "Why am I doing this? Why should I work hard at school, or anything, when the truth is I don't think I'm gonna make it to be 18?"

It wasn't until another death of a close friend that I sank into a deep state of depression. I just wanted to be heard but no one would listen to me. It seemed like no one wanted to hear about what was really going on in my life, especially at the school I attended, where the kids were more secluded from the violence wreaking havoc on my community. Ironically, the Monday after the murder of my friend, I walked into class and my teacher asked us to pull out a pencil and paper and gave us and assignment to write a poem about anything we felt we wanted others to hear. For the first 30 minutes of class I wrote nothing because I could not think of anything I wanted my classmates and teacher to know other than the pain I was feeling.

I finally decided to begin writing and once I started I couldn't hold back. I was still freshly traumatized by the death of my friend over the weekend so I started my poem right there. The next day we were asked to read what we had written. One by one we walked up and I remember waiting to read because I knew once I did my life was going to change. I knew people would look at me differently, so I sat back and watched a few girls get up and read poems about their favorite boy band, worst heartbreak, and flowery stories about trips to Aspen and Cancun. Out of nowhere my teacher asked me if I was ready to read my poem. I hesitantly walked up to the front of the class and took a deep breath and started to read:

Last night I saw my homie shot and killed in the streets man

But I didn't see nobody walking the streets mad and protestin'

Seems like we need to spend more black on black time

 Focusing on black on black crime,

'Cause it seems like the only time that we love the brother man

Is when he is killed by the hands of the other man

Then we stand up and talk about thangs that we can't stand

But if we can't stand up for injustices done to our people by our people

Should we expect to be considered equal?

I don't think so and a lot of my peoples don't think,

So we end up in a state of ignorance that is bliss

I'm trying to get my people to get on the bus

But we always late so we just miss

And then we wonder why we suffer through all of these great crises

Maybe 'cause we don't understand how great Christ is

They say if we take one step, He will take two

But we too busy complaining and singing the blues

Allowing our youth to claim this thug life

But how dare we let them claim thug and life in the same breath

Cause to be a thug is to be allowed to mentally physically, and spiritually to kill yourself

With no life left but just our mamas tears rolling on caskets

Daddy's son wrapped in plastic, little brothers left to raise themselves

All while we holla thug life as we take our last breath

But I choose not to preach to the choir

I would rather go out to the streets and preach to
the kids
Helping them to reach for something higher
You know like helping them to fill out job
applications and school registrations
Speaking from my heart and not just for self-
gratification
Those are some of the real issues dealing with this
nation
Issues dealing with this nation, issues dealing with
this nation
Let me ask you this: "Is you dealing with this
nation?"
Cause man we got drug dealings and drive by
killings in my hood
And y'all its devastating and the murderer of my
homie
Continues to walk the streets
So for Justice we are still waiting,
For justice we are still waiting

Man it's just us and we are still waiting.

The whole time I read not one person moved. For that matter no one seemed to even take a breath. Unlike the other kids who received claps and cheers after their poems, the class was dead silent after I finished. As I folded up my poem and walked back to my seat I remember feeling as if I was in the classroom by myself. The only time I had ever felt so isolated is when I was placed in Special Education back in elementary school.

To add to the pain I felt, after class I received a message that I needed to come to the office. When I walked in my teacher was standing there with the school psychologist who was attempting to speak with me, making me feel like I was "crazy". At least that's what everyone thought about people who were sent to the "school shrink" as we called him. I had been hurting for a while but continued to show up to school because I had a lot of dreams I wanted to accomplish. After this experience, I could no longer put up with what I felt was the nightmarish, abusive relationship I had with school. So after my meeting with the physiologist I felt that I only had one choice. Instead of heading back to class I took the long walk down the hallway towards the exit doors, pushed them open and walked away from school. I had officially decided that I was dropping out.

THINGS I WISH MY TEACHER KNEW

I wish my teacher knew that what I wanted more than anything was to feel like my classroom was a safe space to talk about my reality and my experiences.

At my relatively affluent school, it was not surprising that most of the students' poems were about wonderful childhood experiences, expensive vacations, and puppy love. My teacher and classmates were perfectly comfortable engaging with these poems, clapping, asking questions, giving feedback, and encouragement. My classmates could share their realities without judgement. Even though my experiences may not have been reflective of their realities, I wanted the same courtesy. I wanted my teacher to ask me questions about my experience, or at the very least, say something – anything – to make me feel like I was not completely alone. Honestly, if she had done this, I might have been more open to having a conversation with the school psychologist. If she had asked me if I wanted to talk to someone, rather than ambushing me like I had done something wrong, I may not have felt like my school would never understand me or be able to meet my unique needs.

ENGAGEMENT APPROACH

"The core experiences of psychological trauma are disempowerment and disconnection from others. Recovery, therefore, is based upon the empowerment of the survivor and the creation of new connections. Recovery can take place only within the context of

relationships; it cannot occur in isolation."(Herman, 1992/1997).

Recovery from trauma will occur best in the context of healing relationships. For a child to have a positive view of him or herself reflected in the eyes of a trusted, caring adult counteracts the negative internal view he or she has and heals the terrifying experience of abuse. (Commissioner, VCS, 2007).

As teachers we will inevitably encounter kids who have experienced some type of trauma. The last thing we want to do is further traumatize them with our reactions to their experiences. Teachers are not school counselors, and schools have counselors for a reason, but it doesn't take a counselor to be empathetic and supportive. If a student shares an experience with you, honor the trust they have placed in you by first letting them know that you appreciate them sharing with you, let them know that you care about what happened to them, and then offer help or resources, such as counseling if they are open and ready to receive them. If they are not ready, let them know that you care by providing them with a listening ear.

Research on traumatized children has found that some of the key elements of overcoming trauma are: 1) the adults in their lives acknowledging the trauma they have faced, 2) appropriate nurturing, and 3) letting them know that we care (Commissioner, VCS, 2007). By not speaking to me about my poem at all and then calling me to the office, my teacher made me feel as if she had dismissed my feelings outright. If she could applaud a student and ask them questions about their trip to Cancun, why couldn't she ask questions about an issue that was clearly very important to me? She could have at least acknowledged my pain and said something kind and encouraging. Instead she stigmatized me and made me feel even more isolated.

SUMMARY

Working with students who have experienced trauma is difficult. It can even be scary when the trauma they experience is unfamiliar to us or seems overwhelming. Teachers cannot solve all of the problems of their students and they should not be expected to do so. What can be reasonably expected is that teachers, as trusted and caring adults, will provide an empathetic listening ear and acknowledge the feelings. It's really that simplistically difficult. In summary, we should remember:

- When students open up to us and share a piece of their lives with us, we owe it to them to listen, acknowledge their feelings, and make them feel safe.

- Before offering resources such as counseling or special programming to students who are having difficulty, first of all, do not offer resources without first offering your empathy, then have a conversation with them. Your students are individuals with rights, agency, and personal autonomy. They should be included in decisions about counseling, therapy and other kinds of intervention. Failing to do so alienates and isolates students who are already fragile.

REFERENCES

1. Bell, C. C., & Jenkins, E. J. (1991). Traumatic stress and children. *Journal of health care for the poor and underserved*, 2(1), 175-185.

2. Bell, C. C., & Jenkins, E. J. (1993). Community violence and children on Chicago's southside. *Psychiatry*, 56(1), 46-54.

3. Commissioner, V. C. S. (2007). Calmer classrooms: A guide to working with traumatised children.

4. Herman, Judith (1992/1997) Trauma and Recovery: The Aftermath of Violence – From Domestic Abuse to Political Terror. Basic Books, New York.

12th Grade

It Only Takes One Teacher to Make a Difference

"You don't get an education so you can leave your community, but rather so you can come back and help your community."

After dropping out of school my life started spiraling out of control, and the violence around me increased as I spent more time with my friends who were caught up in gangs and the drug game. It wasn't long after I left school that I got caught up in my own dilemma when I was busted for boosting clothes from the store I worked for. It had only been four months since I dropped out of school and now I was on my way to jail.

While in jail I started truly reassessing my life and searching for my peace and place in the world. I knew that the only way this was going to happen was if I learned how to forgive those who had hurt me and most importantly, I needed to forgive myself. After a lot of soul searching and time alone I knew I was on the right path to healing. Upon my release I had a few decisions to make. Should I go back to the hood and run with my homies or should I give school one more try? As I have written about in my book *The Dropout*, my best friend Joey was the one responsible for motivating me to give school another try. When I returned, it was not the school work that was my biggest hurdle to overcome; it was the teachers who were holding my past against me.

The first day of school was surreal. I felt I like I

had aged so much after spending a year away. I was no longer the same person. It had been a while since I still had some innocence because of the environment where I grew up. But after leaving and spending almost a year running the streets with gangs, getting into trouble and spending time in jail, I had become a little more hardened than before. In my mind I had become an adult after my loss of innocence. The choice to come back to school which was the place that I felt was my abuser and submit myself to their rules and regulations was not easy, especially after having a taste of incarceration and what I thought was freedom after dropping out. But returning was something that I felt I needed to do. When many of my friends asked me why I was returning I didn't have a clear reason to give them, but I knew something was waiting for me so I figured I would show up until I found my answer.

The first couple of days back were very awkward as many of my teachers questioned my presence when they saw me. Over and over again, I had to explain that

I was officially back and prove that I had officially changed. I felt like a few of them were out to get me and would not give me a chance no matter what. But for the most part the vast majority of my teachers were there to help me. This is a revelation that I developed during my time out on the streets. I had run through my mind over and over again the help that many of my teachers had offered up and came to the conclusion that although most of them had very limited knowledge of how to help me, that did not mean that they didn't care.

As mentioned in my book *The Dropout* of all the people who ended up reaching out to me the most during my time of need was a police officer. He shared with me a conversation he overheard some teachers having about me as they were betting on if I would make it to graduation. He just wanted to let me know he believed in me and was pulling for me. This experience was one I would never forget, as I began to see that not everyone was my enemy. My life was truly coming full circle.

Throughout the year I accomplished many of the goals I sat out to accomplish. I rejoined the football team that I was once the star for, and started receiving offers to come play in college. I also ended up winning the state title in wrestling as written about in my book, *Wrestling for My Life.* On the surface things looked like they were going great for me. But behind the scenes I was extremely lonely, sad and in a constant state of fear, because I didn't know if I would emotionally or physically survive the year. In order for me to graduate from school I would have to endure the long road ahead of me. This path was paved with the war happening in my neighborhood, the war that was being waged against us by many of the police officers, and then there was the night, weekend and summer school that I would have to complete just to walk across stage. Outside of sports, inside of my house was the only place where I found comfort, but being home was often difficult too, because there was seldom food to eat and often our utilities were cut off.

Many days I contemplated leaving for good, but I would always think about the promise I made to myself. I had vowed that no matter how hard it got or how mad I got, I would see this thing through, because I had something to prove to everyone and myself.

For many of my teachers, once they saw me working as hard as I could they did their best to encourage me, but because I was living such a different life than most of my classmates I needed different answers. As I struggled through my classes during the year, they all told me over and over again that if I was able to graduate I would be able to get out of my neighborhood for good, as if that was my reward for finishing school. I understood that they saw the news reports of the killing and violence, so they thought that they were doing the right thing by encouraging me to leave.

Of all the teachers I had, there was just one in particular whose voice stood out because she was saying something different. Ms. A. was a middle aged white lady who made it a point to talk to me about life outside of school. She always asked me a question about things going on in my life and neighborhood, and then followed up with the question that haunted me all year: "What are you going to do about it?" At first her question threw me off because it sounded like she was being condescending. But she kept asking me the same question every time we had a conversation. So I finally decided to ask her why she continued to ask me this question.

She said, "Well, I know a lot of people think you should leave your neighborhood forever but I personally feel like once you get your education you should come back. Joseph I want you to know that I see you becoming a great leader for your people in your community, but you have to realize this for yourself and that will only come when you understand the responsibility you have to get your education and give it back."

Words have never rung so true to me. It was then that I began to see my journey as something bigger than myself. She helped to connect what I felt was my calling to help the youth in my community one day. She showed me how all of the challenges I was going through would be useful for a lifetime of service. This was the answer I was in search of, what I had come back to school to get, the answer to the questions I had while lying in my jail cell, and the answer to the pain I saw in my community. Helping me to connect the dots served as a major turning point in my life and educational path. School became much more relevant and my goal to get out into the world and help others pushed me through the lonely and sad moments.

Months later after spending years as a kid labeled as "Special Ed", learning disabled, oppositional defiant, inattentive ADD, illiterate, at risk, troubled, angry, depressed, juvenile delinquent, jail bird and high school dropout, I walked across stage as a high school graduate. Although I was ranked last in my class, it did not stop me from feeling a sense of accomplishment. Afterwards, Ms. A. found me and gave me the biggest hug and kiss on the cheek, then whispered in my ear, *"You are going to change the world"*.

THINGS I WISH MY TEACHER KNEW

I wish my teachers knew that "getting out" is not always the goal.

A study that examined the perception of "success" among African American parents found that the two keys were that, 1) their children would get an education then move home to give back to the community, and 2) their children would work in their communities to support their community and their family (Farmer et al., 2006). While encouraging students to "get out" may be well intentioned, teachers should consider that this advice is not always culturally relevant or acceptable. Many students and their families see improving their neighborhoods as a high priority and a desirable goal.

Teachers should also be mindful not to speak disparagingly about the communities they teach in – the communities that their students call home. While you may enter a community and see blight and poverty, there is also so much more that lies beneath. The couple who has lived in the neighborhood for 50 years, the woman who babysat generations of children, the people your students know and love. Helping students to see how their education connects to the goal of giving back to their community might inspire and motivate many of your students to work hard so that they can have an impact on the communities they love. It gives them a purpose that is bigger than themselves.

I wish my teacher knew that students who have had adult experiences and responsibilities may need schools to adopt special and creative approaches to

educating and interacting with them.

After returning to school I found that there were very few resources to support students like myself. As I mentioned in this chapter, coming back to school and submitting to the same rules and regulations as the kids who were numerically and experientially younger than me was extremely tough. For example, earlier in the year I was denied a request to leave and go to the restroom when I really needed to go. I recognize my teachers may have felt like they were teaching me a lesson on how the real world works, but I had already been out in the real world and experienced what it was like to have the freedom to go to the restroom without permission.

I started understanding why so many of my peers had decided that school was not for them. It was not because they did not value education; it was mainly because they felt like education did not value them. My peers and I had a lot of other real life responsibilities and realities that made getting an education less of a priority. Many of them had grown out of school. We were being forced to negotiate living two totally different lives. In one life we had to choose if we wanted to go to school for our future, in the other we had choose to if we wanted to survive in the present. At home we were often charged with more adult responsibilities like taking care of younger family members, many of whom were our own children and siblings because of the addictions, absences and struggles of our parents. We were also forced to bear the weight of providing money so our families could eat, although the money we made was sometimes made illegally because we often could not get hired. We were just kids but we were forced to keep our guards up as we also became the protectors of our families.

Many of us were also battling with substance and drug addictions, repeat incarceration, and mental health issues. We dealt with the trauma of having our innocence ripped from us and thrown into an adult world where we had to be on constant guard, only to come to school and be asked to conform and submit by making ourselves completely vulnerable, and this was difficult. In my case I was able to work within the expectations, but it never stopped me from questioning if those expectations were realistic and who they were meant for. I also had an expectation that my teachers should teach me and help prepare me for the real world. For this to happen, I should have been given more real world opportunities. I needed less nightly homework and more project based assignments where I could use real world problem solving skills. And this was not for just math, but for all subjects.

I wish my teacher knew that addressing my concerns outside of class in the classroom was an important part of keeping me engaged in school.

Outside of the conversations I had with Ms. A., the problems in my community were never discussed in any of my classes. If I had been given more assignments that allowed me to address problems in my community I would have never dropped out. I would have run to school every day. If I had service opportunities in my community, this would have given me more peace and that peace would have helped me focus better on the tests my teachers said were so important. Instead, most of the learning that was taking place was all in the name of helping me to be prepared for a future that I was uncertain I would live to see.

I wish my teacher knew every child will not go to college – and the ones who don't, deserve to receive education and information that will prepare them for their future too.

There was so much emphasis on everyone going to college that the kids who had no desire to go were alienated. Many of them remained silent about not wanting to attend because they did not want to be seen as not valuing education. Honestly, if it were not for my dreams to play football and becoming a community servant I would have not gone to college either.

The "college or bust" culture was well intentioned but bad in implementation. We were never asked what we wanted to do. I personally felt that they should have introduced us to more fields that did not require college attendance, but rather required a certification or trade school where we could have a career and make money to provide for our families more quickly. It often felt as if our school was playing games with our lives, pushing us to college even if we were not ready just so they could sit back and brag about how many of their students they got into college. They were playing this game at the expense of what was best for us. Because I had some unique experiences there should have been more opportunities and options for me to explore.

ENGAGEMENT APPROACH

As busy as we are as teachers, it is imperative that we individualize education for our students – or at the very least, make sure we take each students individual circumstances into account. Not all students have the goal of leaving their community. Imagine if we found ways to create opportunities for our students to give back to their community. Rather than giving nightly worksheets that encourage memorization, we can design creative individual and group projects that require critical thinking and involve an element of service.

Not all students desire to go to college. It is our job to do our very best to prepare students for life after school. In order to do that we should be sure to include discussions with our students about careers they can pursue that require certifications or trade school. If you have a student who wants to be an electrician for example, provide information and resources that give that student information about how to go about this. Also, understand that it is not important that every student know exactly what they want to do after high school. Many students need a period of self-discovery and maturation to decide what they are really passionate about. Even students, who are convinced of what they want to do, change their minds. The key here is to expose students to a variety of options and to encourage kids to plan for their future.

As I stated earlier, students who have had adult experiences or who have adult-like responsibilities require us to think differently about how we engage them in the classroom. The student who is also a parent may have difficulty submitting to rules designed to keep children in check. For example, students with children should not be expected to turn off their cell phone because they may need to be reached in case of an emergency with their kids.

When I was a senior in high school, I had a job, an apartment, and paid my own bills. Some kids are the primary caregiver for younger siblings and/or elderly family members. I am not saying that the rules should not apply, I am simply suggesting that, 1) we should be aware of who these students are, and, 2) we should have individualized rules, disciplinary plans, and lesson plans for these students.

SUMMARY

Being aware of our student's circumstances, desires, and viewpoints takes time. It is also imperative that we do this. It allows us to be the most effective teachers and mentors we can possible be because our students will trust that we care about their lives and their communities. As we go into the classrooms, remember:

- Get to know your students. Ask them how they feel about college, ask them about their lives, and ask them about their definition of success. As educators, we have to be willing to partner with our students to ensure that they get what they need from their education. We can't do that if we won't take the time to understand their lives.

- Not all kids want to "get out". They may want to have a better life and overcome bad circumstances, but they may also desire to stay in their communities and help the people they love do the same. Be sensitive to these students and their sense of community. Negating this feeling or trying to convince them that this is not a good choice will only alienate them and give them the impression that you don't care about their lives or do not understand the importance of giving back. This will be detrimental to your ability to truly connect with them.

- Try your best to know which of your students may require a different kind of interaction to be successful in school because of special circumstances like being a parent or caregiver, having spent time in jail or juvenile detention or having a parent in prison or on drugs. These students will need special consideration. Beyond just interacting differently with them, they may need more time to complete assignments, tutoring, or weekend classes. Be aware and open so that all of your students can succeed.

Know that if you suggest to a kid that leaving and never coming back is the definition of success, you may be contributing to the lack of resources and leadership that already exists in many underserved communities.

REFERENCES

1. Farmer, T. W., Dadisman, K., Latendresse, S. J., Thompson, J., Irvin, M. J., & Zhang, L. (2006). Educating Out and Giving Back: Adults'

Conceptions of Successful Outcomes of African American High School Students from Impoverished Rural Communities. *Journal of Research in Rural Education*, 21(10), 1-12.

2. Finn, J. D. (2006). The adult lives of at-risk students: The roles of attainment and engagement in high school: Statistical analysis report.